ROCK PAPER **SEX**

BREAKWATER
P.O. Box 2188, St. John's, NL, Canada, A1C 6E6
WWW.BREAKWATERBOOKS.COM

A CIP catalogue record for this book is available from Library and Archives Canada.
Copyright © 2017 Kerri Cull
ISBN 978-1-55081-671-6

We acknowledge the support of the Canada Council for the Arts, which last year invested $153 million to bring the arts to Canadians throughout the country. We acknowledge the financial support of the Government of Canada and the Government of Newfoundland and Labrador through the Department of Tourism, Culture, Industry and Innovation for our publishing activities.
PRINTED AND BOUND IN CANADA.

The opinions expressed in this book are those of the interviewees and participants and do not necessarily represent the opinions of the publisher or author. There is no assurance that any legal statement contained herein remains accurate or precise as laws are subject to change.

Breakwater Books is committed to choosing papers and materials for our books that help to protect our environment. To this end, this book is printed on a recycled paper that is certified by the Forest Stewardship Council®.

MIX
Paper from
responsible sources
FSC® C016245

Second Printing 2017

ROCK
PAPER
SEX

THE OLDEST
PROFESSION
IN CANADA'S
OLDEST CITY

KERRI CULL

TO THE BRAVE PARTICIPANTS
WHOSE NAMES I CANNOT LIST,
THANK YOU
FOR TRUSTING ME WITH YOUR STORIES.

FOR

TRUDY-ANN SINGH AND KELLY FLYNN

There's a thousand shades of white
and a thousand shades of black
but the same rule always applies
smile pretty, and watch your back.
– Ani Difranco, "Every State Line"

The margins are shifting.
The crisis was never one of morals,
but of money.
– Melissa Gira Grant, *Playing the Whore: The Work of Sex Work*

Contents

Introduction

THE CBC ARTICLE READ, "Gang rape warning issued for St. John's sex workers." Sex workers were going to a hotel thinking they would be servicing one individual only to find themselves forced into a room with anywhere between twelve and twenty men. No one was arrested. No official complaints were made. The Safe Harbour Outreach Project released a red alert to warn other sex workers. Articles ran in *The National Post*, *The Globe and Mail*, on *Reddit* and *Vice*. And then the news cycle continued, and everyone seemed to forget about it. Where were the victims' voices in the articles I was reading? I couldn't find any. I found perspectives from law enforcement and outreach personnel, but nothing from a victim. What followed over the next few months were more media articles and investigations about sex work in St. John's, and rarely did they showcase the voice of anyone involved on the ground level. I started reading.

In *Sex Workers in the Maritimes Talk Back*, Leslie Ann Jeffrey and Gayle MacDonald confirmed my suspicions. Their research shows that between 1986 and 2002 the most commonly published voices on sex work in Atlantic Canada were police officers followed by politicians, government workers, lawyers, and then judges, leaving only fifteen percent of the information coming directly from sex workers (155). With that in mind, I committed to exploring the sex trade in St. John's. I had no intel and no definitive objective. Just questions. Questions that led me to the beginning of this project. I had no idea what I was getting into.

When I first endeavoured to write this book, I had very different plans. I would interview sex workers. I would write their stories. I would tell it like they told it. I would bear witness. Little did I know that my opinions and assumptions would be stretched and modified each time I sat down to talk with someone. Little did I know that the landscape of language with which I chose to discuss this project would be difficult terrain to navigate, and that one person's story and perspective would be vastly different from the next.

Conducting the research was the easy part. I posted ads, talked to anyone who would talk to me, and read every book and article I could find. I just wanted all the stories. From stories of sadness and survival to stories of empowerment and love, every interview was different. Every interview taught me more and more about what it's like to be a person trying to get through the world with whatever knowledge and experience we have behind us. I learned something from each individual, and, if the interview was conducted in person, I usually had a good time and felt truly connected to the subject by the time it ended, which resulted in partnerships that allowed me to successfully finish this project. Most of these partnerships started with an email or the answering of an ad that slowly progressed into a lengthy email exchange. The participants would usually interview me. Most, naturally, didn't trust me at first, thought I was a secret-revealing journalist who wouldn't respect them or the way they wanted to be portrayed. One even accused me of being an undercover cop. It often took a long time to build trust before we could freely talk. Once the interview was complete I would go home and transcribe it myself, being sure to promptly delete the audio recording. After writing each piece, the participant would review my work to ensure I told their story as they saw it.

And out of respect for each participant's individual voice and experience, I incorporate different terms and expressions throughout this book to describe the work. Some subjects refer to themselves as prostitutes, others as sex workers, survivors, or service professionals. I utilize the language of their perspective to best tell their story and reflect their attitude. Many take offence to *prostitute* because it conjures stereotypical images of women on the street in miniskirts, addicted to one narcotic or another. The term often makes victims feel as if they somehow had a choice in their victimization and deepens their shame. It makes women who sell their services by choice feel degraded. *Sex worker* is equally offensive to some. A woman, man, child, or teenager forced to sell their body for any reason or by any person is not a worker; they are victims. There are many sex workers out there, however, who feel empowered by that title. They are working, selling something that is their own and that no man, government, or law should have a right to control.

While this book is, on the surface, about sex work, it's really about individuals who have never told their stories. Real people with experiences, lives, stresses, opinions, hobbies, bills, feelings, and goals. More often than not, the details of their lived experiences dispel the uninformed stereotypes which plague public opinion. Understanding those lived experiences can lessen the silencing effects of stigma.

It's important to note that I purposefully did not seek or include stories on human trafficking or child sexual slavery. Human trafficking and child prostitution are black-and-white issues in that they are not the results of personal choice or autonomous adult decision making. While some participants have been in forced situations in the past, they are not at this time. They are currently on the other side of that life. Everyone interviewed in this collection is over the age of twenty and has come to this life in different ways. That being said, I was committed to researching all aspects of the sex trade and conducted quite a bit of research on human trafficking. Resource and reference information is included toward the end of the book. I've also included some information on various organizations that work to support sex workers, women, victims, and others. Many of these organizations accept different forms of donations, not just the traditional monetary kind.

Individuals you will meet in this collection include a stripper who has had nearly $30,000 worth of plastic surgery to make her body perfect in her eyes, a transgender sex worker who finds sex work gender confirming, a dominatrix who is a BDSM lifestyle consultant, a john whose marriage recently disintegrated due to his philandering, a man who has availed of services from high-end escorts and massage parlours, a woman who was forced into prostitution as a teenager, a suburban couple who offers erotic massage from their family home, a sex worker who was victimized by multiple men in a hotel room, a divorced mother who works in a massage parlour, a sex worker who summarizes some of her weirdest clients, a stripper who identifies as a feminist, an escort who is a highly educated woman with a powerful day job, and more. Between chapters there are some lone, anonymous quotations from interested participants who did not want to have their stories told entirely but had opinions or perspectives they wanted to share. They are all from sex workers.

Other participants include a manager of a local strip club and some others who work on the periphery of the sex industry plus some perspectives from outreach and legal personnel. In most cases, names and other identifying information have been changed to protect the participants. It's important to note that each participant has signed off on the publication of their story.

Naturally, reader discretion is advised. These essays contain sexual and graphic language that some may find offensive.

"Drug dealers walk up and down the street all day. One man is old, like grandfather old, and he does what he wants with the girls because he has drugs. It's **disgusting."**

Kicking was the Whole Point

IT WAS A BUSY Saturday in October. The Tim Hortons was packed. Children at the next table were yelling nonsense syllables. Three thin guys who looked to be in their twenties donning white baseball hats and thin moustaches sipped medium coffees at the table behind us. A senior in a black fur coat and matching tam ambled to the table near the window holding a raisin tea bun on a small plate.

Lori asked me to get her a small Iced Capp. I thought about the type of woman that would order a small Iced Capp in mid-October. Who drinks a cold, beige, syrupy coffee-like substance when there's frost on the ground? Truth be known, I didn't really understand her. I balanced the paper-covered straw atop the plastic lid and pushed it to the other side of the table.

Her eyeliner was perfect. That's the first thing I noticed. And I mean perfect. It would take me hours and multiple tries to get that seamless liquid line. She said it took her five hours to learn how to do it right.

Lori's been doing in-calls at her apartment for about a year, an apartment she shares with her boyfriend and his friend. Last night was busier than usual. The thin girls get most of the business on the weekends, but last night, Lori actually had to turn people down, which is rare. Lori's busiest times are Tuesday to Friday after 4pm, lunch times, and around Christmas. She said husbands sometimes use the excuse that they have to go Christmas shopping to hook up.

Lori emphasizes that the work itself is nothing like she thought it would be:

> It's nuts. Before I started doing this I thought, *oh my god, it's so dangerous. So and so does it and she's going to get stabbed.* It's not like that at all. Not nearly. I'm sure places are very dangerous, but here it's not. The guys are so good.

She did work from a car once (what people in the industry call "car dates") but has never worked from the street, which would obviously bring more risks. Lori admits she would not have enough nerve to work from the street. She refers to the women downtown who work outside: "They either need it bad or they got a lot of nerve. I would never... it's like going to The Cotton Club and getting on the stage. Balls of steel."

The journey into sex work started when she became tired of her minimum-wage job that offered minimal hours. She never thought she'd actually get into this life. It wasn't on her radar. Then a friend showed her the website *NL Adult*. They were laughing about it, making fun of what people were asking for in terms of services.[1] What she found most surprising was the amount of money people were getting for doing little things. Later on that week she was stressing about bills and rent. She was always a bit promiscuous, she admits, so she felt it wasn't a big leap for her. She vowed that it would be only this one time, and when job hours were cut, Lori decided to try it.

That first date came pretty fast.

> It was pouring out. I was in leggings and boots. I had a friend stand outside the house and wait for me. I walked out with $100 for forty minutes. Since then I haven't worked, I haven't had a full-time job in nine

---

1   I randomly selected four Saturdays over the course of a year to see what kind of services were being offered and requested on the site. Much of it was run-of-the-mill requests like male seeking male or male seeking female for a fun time. There were some others that didn't sit well with, I'd assume, the general browser such as "Man Seeking Woman for Daddy Daughter Rape Fantasy" and a woman looking for "A Man and His Beast."

months. Like it's paid for my Christmas last year. It's crazy. The money is wicked.

Just recently, Lori was considering giving it up and going back to regular work, and she cringed at the thought. No money. Back to nothing. It was not something she was seriously considering. "My rent is paid in full. My credit cards are paid off. It's crazy. That's why you do it. You have to be a certain type of person to do this." Sometimes she loves it, and sometimes she hates it, but for her, the pros outweigh the cons.

So what type of person is Lori? She is twenty-five, has moved around quite a bit, but has never been off the island. Everyone in her ex-tended family works in trades or is on social services. She describes herself as a big girl and loves sandwiches. She is a proud bayman. She has cankers due to vaping, which she's using to stop smoking cigarettes. She has mastered the art of applying eye make-up. She loves slippers, cats, and books.

LORI STARTED DOING OUTCALLS but, after the third one, decided it was safer to have johns come to her place. She had an incident where a man asked her to go to his house near the Village Mall in the city's west end. She got on the bus and ventured out. She couldn't find the house, so she texted him and asked for the address again. He gave her directions on where to go and instructions on how to act. Her gut told her something was awry, but he persuaded her to go through with it, promising an extra few bucks in the envelope. The person who answered the door had no clue who she was or what she was there for. It was a prank. She could see his buddies through the window, and they were dying laughing. Apparently they wanted to surprise their friend who was recently single. That was the last outcall Lori ever did. The next night, Lori and her friend got the bus back to the West End, found the house again, and egged it.

Now, she accepts clients in her apartment, which is in a secure build-ing. It's comfortable. She feels safe.[2] People are always coming and

---

2 Even though she feels safe, she has in the past hid knives around her room—one of the benefits of taking clients into her environment.

going so no one notices anything strange happening. Her room-mates leave the apartment, sometimes wait down the hall or outside the door to make sure everything's okay, even though Lori says she's never had problems. "Ninety-nine percent of the guys are great." By that she means they are who they say they are, and they pay as promised. One regular comes over twice a week, braids her hair, gives her a massage, and they talk. It's her favourite type of client—the ones who just need companionship. About forty percent of her clientele are regulars, which is comfortable. Her clients range from ages nineteen to sixty-eight. She says, "Older guys is where it's at" because there's a chance that she might enjoy the session too. "I hate doing young guys. My preferred is thirty-five and up. The young guys, sometimes they're okay. Most times they're not."

She will service almost anyone as long as they're respectful and pay up front. It does take some mental gymnastics to get to that place where she compartmentalizes it as just a job. She needs to get into a certain frame of mind, needs to get into a role-playing mentality, needs a costume, have full make-up on. It's an act.[3] She wants the men to enjoy themselves and she'll try to accommodate them as long as they're not crossing any lines.

Although most guys are respectful, she does deal with some doozies. Like the one who came to her door promising a certain amount of money and then telling her she was worth $30. She threw him out.

Another time, Lori had a big spender call her. He was literally throw-ing money at her as he came in the door, which was overwhelming but welcomed. She didn't feel comfortable having that money in the room, so she brought it to her living room. After they hooked up, he took the cash and left. The second time someone tried that, Lori decided to take matters into her own hands. She tracked him down online and broke up his private relationship. She found his fiancé on social media and asked her for the money for certain sexual services with the john's email correspondence attached.

---

3   Most of the workers I interviewed agreed that this is the way they approach their work. One woman told me she acts more bubbly than her real personality would allow. She tries to be more stereotypically feminine and flirtatious.

One john in particular made her feel uncomfortable. He went around her house to make sure there were no "weird smells" and then made her put up an extra curtain in her bedroom window. He then asked her to pretend to be a fourteen-year-old girl and even brought an outfit for her to wear. She will not see him again.

She was taken advantage of once by a guy who had a yelling fetish. He called her and was saying things to her trying to make her mad, and it worked. She yelled at him, and before she knew what was happening, it was too late.[4] Another time, she discovered a man was using her photos to lure men to his home.

There are some fetishes Lori didn't even know existed. Like smoking. One man came to her house and she was just finishing her smoke as he came in. Not too long after, he had to leave because he had become so aroused by her smoking, he was done. She had no idea.

On another occasion, she was asked to accept a paint detailing gun as payment, the john persisting that she could sell it and make a lot of money. She gave him the benefit of the doubt, and looked into how much she could get for it. She quickly learned it was stolen.

One john came to her house with only $25, which was below the agreed upon price. "Who goes to someone's house with $25 and expects a blowjob? Fuck off and go home out of it."

Bartering is a normal thing in this industry. One guy told Lori her breasts didn't look as big as they did in her photo and wanted to pay less because of it. Lori can shrug off these comments without much care. "They're tits buddy. You got to touch 'em. They don't got any weird moles or hair. I think you did pretty good for yourself."

The strangest request she ever received was to repeatedly kick a man in the testicles. She was uncomfortable doing it, and said she held

---

4   In those situations, when people are being dishonest or trying to scam, workers have the op-portunity to post about it on the adult sites so others can be forewarned. The Safe Harbour Outreach Project (SHOP) also has a Warn Other Workers (WOW) line which is listed on the resource page toward the end of this book.

back with the first few kicks because it goes against who she is to hurt someone intentionally, but he wanted her to really give it to him. "I was like, are you going to give me money to kick you in the balls? I'll do it." She didn't know what to think of his screams from behind his ball gag, but realized this was something he enjoyed, so she went on with it. She had to increase the volume on the music so the neighbours wouldn't hear. At first she questioned it. How would they have intercourse afterward if he was going to be in so much pain? She didn't know there would be no sex. The kicking was the whole point. He paid her triple the amount he had promised.

Another man wanted to clean her house in the nude while she yelled at him. It was the easiest money she ever made.

Her average clients are working-class types, a lot of construction workers, she says, but there's one client in particular whom she remembers. She said he was basically wearing money. He gave her $200 without even asking her "how much?"

One man was so well endowed she had to turn him away. "You have a lovely penis but it just doesn't go well with me. It's like when women try to fit into a size eight when they're much, much bigger. It goes on, but it shouldn't."

It's not a rare thing that someone will come "just for oral" and then want full service. That's okay in her books. She's fine with using pet names and offering a variety of services, but no cuddling. Cuddling and kissing are reserved for intimate relationships only.

Lori is, above everything else, floored by the amount of attention she gets.

> I'm not everyone's cup of tea. I'm a bigger woman. I'm loud. I'm brutally honest. I got no problem saying no I'm not going to do that. I'm not everyone's preferred body type. If I'm not, that's fine. That's cool. I got no problem with it. For a bigger woman like me to not only get attention but to have men pay for it… It feels

good. Oh man, it does. When I first started I never
thought anyone ever would and since then my confidence has, like, increased by probably eighty percent.

Although it's good for the ego, she does it mainly for the money.
She comments that her friend who has a child in daycare pays a
small fortune, the equivalent of a two-week minimum-wage paycheck per month. "In one night I can make what people make in a
week."

Even though she enjoys her work and has no major issues with it,
not many others know about it. Two of her friends who asked about
her experiences actually ended up trying sex work. Both have since
quit: one due to having a boyfriend and the other because she
didn't enjoy it.

Whenever Lori feels judged by anyone in her circle or in the media,
she immediately becomes defensive.

> How does it harm you directly? It really means nothing.
> I'm not selling cocaine to school kids. There are a lot
> worse things I could be doing. It's been around forever.
> It's the oldest profession. Get with the fucking times.
> If you can justify watching porn, it's the same thing. I
> am a service provider. Can I give you cancer? No. You
> can disapprove. That's your opinion, but keep it to
> yourself. Just because you feel terrible doesn't mean you
> have to make someone else feel terrible. How does it
> affect you directly? People are so closeminded.

One friend took offence to Lori's decision to sell to married men,
but Lori defends her choices. "If you think about it, I'm saving the
marriage; I'm keeping the spark. He probably just needs something
different right now. People are not meant to be monogamous.
I'm not the one that's married. It's not my issue." Sometimes she'll
notice rings. Sometimes guys will take them off, which has nothing
to do with her, but with their own guilt. One customer justified his
choices because he didn't believe oral sex was considered cheating.

Lori disagrees.

She's not afraid to voice her opinions to any of her johns and feels empowered when she does so. She used to be a pushover, couldn't say no to anyone, and she's changed. She has "nerves and balls of steel now." A lot of that nerve comes from the confidence she's gained and the knowledge that she knows what's best for her and her body, what she will and will not risk.

She gets checked for various STDs every month, and always uses condoms for intercourse.[5] She chooses not to use them for oral because "if you're not offering BBBJs, you don't make anything," and they are her bread and butter.[6]

Why anyone would rather not use a condom with a complete stranger, Lori cannot understand. She understands that it feels better, but the risks are just too high. "I am a clean person, but they don't know that. Why would they take the chance? The only reason I think they could risk that is because they already have something. There's something really intimate about that. When you have a spouse, you have to draw the line."[7]

---

5 Lori endorses the Lifestyle brand condom because they're "thicker than a rubber boot" and she has never had one break on her.

6 BBBJ stands for Bare Back Blow Job, which means oral sex without a condom.

7 At the time of publication, Lori was still working out of her home.

"Everyone thinks you're **dirty**.
Everyone thinks you **don't shower**
and you're **homeless**.
I shower **every** fucking day.
·I **don't** have sex with clients ever. **Ever.**
I give blow jobs with **condoms.**
I've **never** had a disease in my life."

I Pay Top Price

WHEN MIKE WAS WORKING in South America in 1980, an older coworker took him to a strip club, and he was offended by the whole situation. He kept returning even though he didn't particularly like it. He used to have an anti-sex-work attitude and even felt he would never get involved in that world. He lost that attitude a few weeks later when a girl approached him at a concert. There were several hours of dancing, and so on, and that attitude left him for good. On his twenty-fifth birthday, he took his first working girl home.

Since then, he has "paid for women a few times," including one "amazing night in Amsterdam." When he met his wife, he left that life behind with the exception of a lap dance every now and then when out for a booze-filled night with friends or coworkers. Twenty-five years passed and due to health problems, sex problems in his marriage, and work-related travel, he made the decision to try an affair if the opportunity arose. For a long time, he thought his wife had some idea about his nights with other women, but nothing concrete.

When trying to meet people out at clubs in 2012, he found that women his age had been burned by unfaithful men and had no interest in dating a married one. Younger women did not care about the fact that he was married, and were more attractive, but generally not interested. Strippers didn't judge him and were very nice to whoever was spending the money.[8]

---

8 Mike had money to burn and would have no problem chucking the $20/lap dance. He would spend hundreds of dollars a night in the strip club.

After travelling the world as part of a lucrative career, he was surprised it took him so long to get propositioned in St. John's. One day he ran into a girl on the street who solicited him, and he brought her to his home. After that he found himself in the strip clubs on a regular basis and met a woman who caused him to rethink what he was doing at the bars with the others. "She did something new to me—she exchanged cell numbers with me. Then she would text me when the club was slow or she was bored." They had a brief relationship. She later returned to her hometown. A year or so later, he contacted her and they started seeing each other regularly.

Since then he has moved around quite a bit, was living in Buffalo for a while and frequented a club where he became popular with the dancers. He would post photos with them on his fake Facebook page, which he used for this part of his life. These social-media actions eventually became industry endorsements for them, and he would befriend the feature girls.[9]

> Travelling entertainers are like everyone else who works on the road. They love to have someone to talk to that can say more than, "I love your boobs." There are serious competitions all over the USA where the top girls wear $5000 costumes and do amazing pole routines and showgirl dancing. The competition is very serious because you can add a championship to your resume and command top appearance fees for several years to follow a win at a top competition.

Mike went into this new interest like he was studying for an exam. He researched the industry, learned about competitive pole dancing, and studied burlesque as well as some aspects of the porn industry.[10] Succeeding in putting his name out there, he was able to attend national competitions and actually talk to performers, which is the

---

9 Feature girls are the performers who have some unique talent. They are the dancers that are incredibly beautiful, have amazing pole skills, or are nationally known porn stars.

10 Having seen burlesque shows in some of the biggest cities in the world, he feels that is what's lacking in adult entertainment in St. John's.

equivalent of getting backstage at a rock show because you're a recognized industry expert or you have friends who are VIPs.

Soon after, he returned to St. John's. The dancers knew him— recognized him. "One of the girls latched on to me immediately and really has been my regular companion for several months. Since most of our meetings are pre-planned, they are very safe for both of us."

Because of his intimate relationship with one or two of the girls, he gets better treatment at the strip bar. "When a girl knows you're there for ten songs they are way more comfortable." They're also more likely to accompany him after the bar closes to a hotel or his apartment. The girls often double up for safety reasons. Even though, Mike says, it's a little more fun, it's not worth the extra money. The women are concerned about diseases and generally carry their own condoms for both vaginal and oral sex, and when the deed is done, they are quick to leave. Mike realizes they want to get back to their own bed and to not be bothered.

Negotiating a price is not something he would ever do. He thinks it's demeaning and humiliating for the women. "I pay top price…say, $500 for a session." He references one woman who comes to St. John's regularly and she charges $300 an hour and that price includes no sex whatsoever.

While there is the exchange of sex and money, which is the crux of the agreement, he says relationships can form, "perhaps completely screwed up but still real." He once met a dancer friend at the Sobeys on Merrymeeting Road who was there with four of her friends. He gave them all a ride home. He also takes the girls to dinner often. "I try to do little things that are very easy to do but mean a lot to them." One woman was in financial need, lost her driver's license, got fired from her dancing gig, and was faced with various fines. He helped her out financially, but confesses it's a moral conundrum:

> If she was working, I'd probably visit her at work and
> end up paying for many dances. Since she isn't working
> I could offer to do a private show. We could do it at a

> hotel and I would expect more sexual activity than at a typical club session. I have done this before with other dancers. The difference here is that we already have a relationship based on conventional friendship. If I ask her to serve me in exchange for the cash she really, really needs, where will that stand? Someone might say I was being a predator taking advantage of her situation. Someone else might say she has already gone down that road by working in a club. I'm not sure which road I will follow.

While many of the girls have a lot of negative stuff in their lives, to his knowledge none of the women he has been with are in big trouble or need serious help. If they appear to be in need, he tries to help them as best as he can, but that gets exhausting both mentally and financially.

The downward turn in the economy and how it will affect the women is of the biggest concern to Mike. Even his most successful friends are finding it tough. In Newfoundland, he attributes part of this problem to the lack of tipping:

> The tipping process does not work in St. John's. In St. John's the girls must make their money in the back rooms. The Cotton Club has one of the best poles in North America, but they very seldom have a girl that can do a show on it. Unfortunately, that great pole seldom gets used because there is no money to be made at the stage. In the US, I have spent several hundred dollars just at the stage. Going on the stage is simply an obligation to the club here. As a result, there is very little enthusiasm shown on stage at all.

The cycle of low tipping and poor stage performance becomes a chicken-and-egg situation.

Even though some of Mike's actions are illegal—paying for sex—he does not really fear the law in Canada even though he admits, "The consequences would be devastating.[11] I could be banned from living in the US and could lose my family and job."

One of the major arguments about legalization of sex work revolves around the risky nature of working on the street. Proponents of legalization suggest that if sex work was legal, it would be out in the open and those who engage in it would have protection, resources, and recourse if they were victimized. Mike agrees that working from the street is risky for both the buyer and the seller.

> I agree with the groups that say the new law does not provide any protection for the girls. I believe that they will have to take more risks because customers will want to hide from the law, and that will force the girls into hazardous situations.

Recently, there was one girl in a desperate situation. He put her up in his apartment for two weeks. While the first few days were fun, things got weird fast. After a stressful flight, her addiction took over, and she popped extra prescription pain pills, but soon after decided she wanted to quit cold turkey. She spent a week managing to be clean. Mike did her grocery shopping and took care of her basic needs during that time until she decided to leave.

While he did his best to support his sex-worker friends, he admits he was sometimes disappointed by their actions. "It may be the oldest profession but they weren't very professional. They were very needy and the excuses for their problems became more and more imaginative." He decided to part ways with the lifestyle and not a moment too soon. His wife had discovered his indiscretions. His spending had increased to tens of thousands of dollars and had become impossible to hide.

With a lawyer's help, she pieced everything together and confronted him with an ultimatum: either he would end it all or she would file for divorce. "This has been the evil side of this industry for

---

11 In Canada now, it is illegal for an individual to purchase sex. For more information on legal matters, see the Q&A at the end of the book.

centuries. But this is all on me. I chose to have these adventures, and blaming the girls for any of this would be ridiculous."

To make matters worse, Mike recently lost his job, which he attributes to the downturn in the economy, but thinks it might have something to do with his unsavoury escapades. "There were a few people in management who heard stories of my adventures and that may have been considered when choosing whom to terminate."

With no money, he quickly faded into the background in the sex industry. He feels blessed that he was able to withdraw from the industry before he lost everything. He has disconnected his phone and only keeps in touch with one woman every now and then, but that too has proved difficult. "Your family will not accept that you only hang with the good ones."

"I only did it **once**.
I will **never** do it again."

The Vagina Monologues

SHIT, SHE FORGOT HER toe rings again. She rounded that bend in the highway that told her she had about a twenty-minute drive left before entering the city limits. She would have to pull over and drive for an hour or more to retrieve the rings from Saul's house. But she had to. She had those toe rings since high school. She swiftly pulled a U-turn, felt the gravel spin up and out around the tires, and peeled back toward the house she had just spent forty-eight hours in, her right hand on the wheel, her left flicking the cigarette butt out the car window, and $2000 in an envelope resting in her bohemian purse on the passenger seat.

When she got back to Saul's, he was playing piano. He jumped when she rounded the corner of the music room.

"I forgot my toe rings."

"They're not here."

He ran his hand through his hair. Glanced at his hands to see if any dye had come off. He had Emily do it for him the day before. The only darkness on his hands were his age spots, which looked like tired polka dots.

She met his eyes and didn't say anything. Strolled through the music room and out the back hallway to the kitchen. She noticed he had just changed the garbage. He followed her. A can of diet ginger ale was open on the counter.

"They're not here."

She knew they were. It wasn't the first time she misplaced them. It wasn't the first time Saul had taken them. She swiftly lifted the bag that was clinging to the side of the white can and there were her two toe rings shining at the bottom like tiny wedding rings.

Her apartment was chilly when she returned that Sunday evening. She immediately turned up the heat to twenty-five, took off her jacket, and flicked the switch on the coffee maker. Her notebook had a blue pen mark across the front. She wrote on page forty-three: "Saul, weekend, 2000." Closed it and then ran the bath.

On the back cover page, she had her price list. What is an hour worth? What would she do for five hundred dollars? What was she worth?

1 hour = $300
2 hours = $500
3 hours = $700
4 hour dinner date (dinner, dessert, two sessions of sex) = $900
Overnight = $1200
Overnight and breakfast = $1800
Full weekend = $2000

SHE DIDN'T GET INTO the game until later in life. Not until she was thirty, which is old for a first go. It wasn't survival sex. It wasn't by choice either. It was somewhere in between. She wanted to make money, good money, in order to live the life she wanted. So she didn't need it for food. She wanted it for good food. There's a difference.

She thought about those first moments when she decided she could do it. *20/20* was profiling the lifestyle of high-end escorting. At that very moment she was living paycheck to paycheck, earning minimum wage at a spa, and living with a girlfriend who had a great job. When her friend went to work she would stay at home and wonder what the hell else she could do to make money. That night while painting her toenails, she listened to the women's stories chronicling adventures and wealth. She could do this.

Could she do this?

Once the decision was made, she went online and researched to see what the industry was like in the city and elsewhere: prices, commentary, and so on. She was looking to be a little different. There were too many sleazy offers online, more than anyone could ever count or want. Upscale was what she wanted to be. A woman for gentlemen. She contacted Deb, the website's owner, and set up a meeting. What was this Deb person going to be like, she wondered. What was someone who did this for a living like?

Over lattes, she quickly realized Deb was not to be messed with. Not an inch of fat. Built for speed. A hard ticket. Emily could tell this woman had been into some shady stuff in her day. Two days later when Emily saw her ad, saw herself posed with back arched and red stilettos adding six inches to her height, she sat back on the couch and exhaled. It looked good. Better than good. "Elite companion available for a fun rendezvous." She liked the sound of that. She was elite. Not a whore or a prostitute. She didn't hate those words, but if a man, a john, referred to her that way, she would feel disrespected.[12]

She would be there to please, to provide immense pleasure, to bring fantasy to life, not to be demeaned or abused. Was she really going to do this. She remembered Debbie's last words before they parted ways after the meeting: "Watch your back." Within two days she had an appointment.

Holy shit. This is happening.

SHE VETTED HER POTENTIAL buyers through an email exchange. The first client was from a Maritime province and around her age. She later would learn that he had a family and discretion was of the

---

12 Nearly everyone I interviewed, with the exception of Emily, disliked the word prostitute.

utmost importance. This is the type of client she preferred—well to do, wealthy, with something to lose.

He seemed polite and could string a sentence together. Rules were hard to come by in this business, but she automatically made a rule for herself that anyone who was crass—using abbreviations, trying to cut her down on price—through the initial email exchange would be kiboshed. She wouldn't even respond to it. *There's Craigslist and Backpages for that and I will never use Backpages*, she thought— another rule that seemed to be manifesting even though it would later be broken.

At first the clients, the money, were all good. Real good. There was one man who owned a company in the US. He was a big wig, a well-known business man. He could not avail of any professional service in his own state. He found her online and they scheduled a trip out of town. The stakes were too high for him to meet Emily in his hometown. This would be her first out-of-town trip. While she was sitting in the airport sipping her coffee, she noticed she was a little shaky. Even though they had seen each other before, this was a new level. This was dangerous. She didn't deny that the nervousness was exciting. She mentally reviewed the items she packed to ensure she wasn't forgetting anything.

He flew her to Montreal in first class, a halfway point between their two cities, where he was attending a conference. She joined him at every event. He introduced her as his girlfriend. They wore uniforms. They ate expensive food. He paid for everything. They walked along the cobblestone streets around old Montreal, went to restaurants. An outsider would definitely accept that they were together in a casual way. When they drove around, she would use the GPS and navigate for him. They had coffee at French cafes. Some might say it was romantic.

When it came to his sexual preferences, he was not so casual. It was nothing she had experienced before. She chalked it up to him watching too much pornography. She remembered him wanting her to just lie there, stiff as a board, almost unnaturally still to the point where her muscles would cramp. She could feel the weight of his wiry body on her. Even when she could hold this position for a long time, it was still hard for him to have pleasure. Porn had ruined him, she thought. Porn is about performance not pleasure.[13]

Over toast and tea the next morning, he admitted it. "'I watch too much porn." Just like that. There's a documentary she saw a couple years ago about a teenager who was addicted to abuse porn, a form of porn that is forceful and violent and sometimes includes "face punishment." She would never stand for anything like that.[14]

While the high-class American business owner was probably the most elite client she had, the old pianist was probably the strangest. He was manic depressive, severely self-medicated, and could not perform, but he still wanted action to the point where she was completely tired. When they would finally try to sleep at around 5am, he would hold her so close, so tight, it was uncomfortable and unnatural. When she'd insist on sleeping on the couch, he would let her do it, but he wouldn't like it. Once he mentioned it in the morning, how it was not what he paid for.

"You need to understand something," she said, "you are paying for my time but all that time is not for me to just rub you out and give myself blisters, that's not healthy for either of us." He never mentioned it again. "He was sweet but crazy, which explains why he wanted my toe rings."

He also gave her a lock of his hair, which, unbeknownst to him, was immediately thrown out. Another gift was an autographed Tony Bennet songbook, which he soon after asked her to return. It was too late because that too had found its home in the dumpster.

---

13 In an essay titled "Myths and Realities of Male Sex Work: A Personal Perspective," River Redwood makes a logical connection between fantasy and reality, noting the danger comes when people forget that porn is not real like when "you see Superman jumping out of a window in a movie, you wouldn't try to emulate it in reality, because you know it's fake and you'd probably end up hurting yourself." While this is an extreme example, it makes the point that pornography is not realistic sex. Problems arise when people deem it so (Van der Meulen, 51).

14 *Hot Girls Wanted* is a documentary produced by Rashida Jones that covers some different aspects of the porn industry, including abuse porn, which is disturbing to say the least. Viewer discretion advised.

SHE THOUGHT ABOUT HOW, in a perfect world, she would run her own house. Not a madam. Being a madam made her think of someone who was walking around in black lingerie, wearing red lipstick and treating everyone poorly, which was not who she was. If she had her time back, she would go into graphic design and learn the ropes, make her own website, live off the avails instead of doing it herself. She would create profiles for girls that would be nice and welcoming, professional and pretty.

> *NL Adult* Classifieds is horrible. Low class. Riff raff. The girls here need someone who knows the industry to create a good site. Not something crass and shitty where dudes are allowed to advertise for "slut buttholes." Forget finding someone that can have a real conversation on that site. I saw a picture earlier today of a woman with this big ass who was bent over. It's not even sexual. It's like I'm going to get my arse wiped by my parents. It's awful.

So if she could go back in time, she would run her own business or return to her twenties again and go about it a bit differently. Travel more to Alberta and British Columbia. Book tours. Get to see places. She knew someone who did that and always thought it would be fun. She would bring her pets. She would have regulars in all of these places.

She never did any tours because other life events got in the way, but she kept at it for a few years before taking some time off due to personal relationships. Then it was off and on "because old habits die hard and the money is killer":

> It's so easy to hardly have to do anything and then get paid a lot of fucking money. When I was working a lot before, I didn't even consider thirty-minute gigs. Now, it's a little different because the economy is failing and it's being felt in every part of the province. It's Mason-jar tight.

The clients want a deal. They often complain that this is too much or they can't afford that. They offer pot. She started doing half-an-hour gigs because it's so hard to get a good client. She chalks it up to *NL Adult* and *Backpages*, describes it as "All shit. Car dates. Right. Yes, b'y. You get picked up. You give someone head in the car. Not a chance. There's no higher tier."

She is not accustomed to that clientele. Her johns are usually married, professional, wanting sex and nothing more. Normal stuff. She thought it was strange that she never had more weird clients. She had a lot of two-hour appointments, which were her favourite. She would push that when people inquired through email: "You know, you'll get more." This means she had fewer clients but more time, and a lot of men can't perform sexually twice in a short amount of time. She would schedule two hours, get some wine, chill, talk about music. "It's not just wham bam thank you man." A rapport is developed and they want to set a second date.

Second and third and fourth dates were the best. There was nothing to fear. Nothing to hide. An odd sense of caring could almost emerge. The risk with single dates and first meetings is the unknown of what lies behind the door. The likelihood that someone could be crazy or deranged.

There was only one time when she felt like something was *off* and curbed her behaviour to protect herself. After arriving at a hotel, she went up in the elevator, and when she got to the floor, she felt like somebody was walking, hurrying away, lurking. She did not actually see anybody. It could have been her imagination. It could have been a ghost. Who knows? She was walking up the hallway, and the closer she got to the room number, the more she realized something was uncomfortable. She turned around and left, emailed him and said she had a car accident, a little fender bender. He was totally normal and reacted well. "It probably wasn't anything, but you have to go with your gut, your instincts. If they say this is not right, don't do it. It would not be a good appointment anyway because you would be second guessing everything."

Emily says, contrary to popular belief, feelings play a role in this industry. Believe it or not, she says, it is not all about sex. Married men had used words like "lonely" and "unappreciated" to describe their feelings in relation to their personal relationships. It was not just about sex, but companionship. It is usually a mutually beneficial agreement.

> I have learned much about myself; I do not trust easily. Never have. People are people. I'll talk to anyone, I don't judge, and people need human connection. It's not just about sex. It's not just about infidelity. And relationships sometimes are cold. There's no touching, there's no loving or affection, and everyone needs that. If they're not getting it at home, nine chances out of ten, they're going to go somewhere else to get it. I know damn straight that I would.

Emily says she knows herself well. More now than ever before. She can do anything she wants if she puts her mind to it. It's all a matter of perspective. "Some people would be like, *I'd never be able to do that, it's crazy*. It's all how you look at it. If you look at it as work, not mixing it. I also learned that I'm a really good liar. I think I already knew that, but it's hard." She's been living a double life. She had to make up a pretend boss, a pretend job, a pretend schedule to talk to her girlfriends, her parents, to explain where her money came from, where her gifts came from, and she finds it hard to lie all the time but gives in to the idea that "you do what you gotta do" because the money is really good. She did learn that she was strong and that she is capable of taking care of herself, getting on her own two feet. "When push comes to shove, you do what you gotta do."

It's either make money this way or be reliant on someone else, and she neither considers nor accepts that possibility. Although she can explain away the reasons why she lies, it takes its toll: "It fucking sucks, messes with your head, you're constantly paranoid. If there's someone to talk to then fine, one can be who they are, but for me,

I felt like if people found out, I would be ruined. Everything. It would be the end of my family, my friendships."

From a small town, she would never even want to go back. It would be the end. She has anxiety and is on medication, but she's unsure if her anxiety is linked to the way she makes money. "Physically I'm fine except for the perpetual UTI. All the time. UTI. UTI. Knowing that I'm susceptible to them, I try to avoid risky situations such as hot-tub sex."

While she takes precautions to protect her physical health, is in near perfect shape, and looks after her appearance, she doesn't have any hard-and-fast rules regarding what she would and would not do. The most important thing is protecting her identity and not showing too much of her real personality. Exposing the real person, the real name, the real family, etc., was her biggest fear. Some of her clients could figure it out, though, particularly if they developed a comfortable, trusting relationship. She would sometimes slip and use her birth name by accident. But discretion was important to the clients too. They often had wives and children they could potentially lose if found out. Then it happened. She was unexpectedly outed and felt as though her life was ruined, but those who knew were understanding and gave her insight into some things they already surmised. A private person, somewhat guarded on a regular day, she was devastated, but now she's glad they know and finds it therapeutic and relieving. Something she never thought she'd feel.

She still hates the individual who outed her and will never talk to that person again. She feels as though something was taken from her that was her secret to tell.[15] "It's hard to even think about if or when you could be outed."

She ran into a regular client once at a performance of *The Vagina Monologues*. "Of all places, right?" He was there with his wife. He saw Emily. He kept looking over. "Hello. Are you enjoying *The*

---

15 This is often the biggest fear of any sex worker—that they will be outed by someone. Even those who feel empowered and freed by their choices usually have one or two people in their lives that don't know.

Vagina Monologues or what? Wicked." Another time, she ran into a john at the university. He just walked right past her. She didn't have any make-up on and thought he didn't recognize her.

She tries not to think about the fact that they could have wives or families. If she started thinking that way, she would go into a downward spiral, so she talks herself out of it. "What is the point? It's just going to hurt. Why go there? Why even put the perspective in my mind? It's a job. I was not the one to take the vow." The only person she really thinks about with concern is the older gentleman who was mentally ill, who gave her the odd gift. She wonders if he's in trouble. She also thinks about another guy that she ended up dating. He was foreign. She fell for him and he for her. They still talk from time to time.

She told her most serious boyfriend about it all. They met on the dating website *Plenty of Fish*. Before she slept with him, she convinced him to watch a movie with her about high-end escorting, an indie film set in New York with the subject making $10,000 a week. She watched his reaction out of the corner of her eye.

> One night I decided I had to tell him. So during a regular dinner-and-movie date, I leaned in and said, "Remind me to tell you something later. It's important." We ended up watching the rest of the show and went back to my house. We laid in bed and I told him. "You know the movie we watched the other night," I said, "what would you do if I was doing that?"

They talked it over and he was hurt because she was lying, but he did not take issue with the work.

After their relationship dissolved, she began dating someone new. She trusts her new partner and told him the truth almost immediately. While he understood, he threatened that he was pretty savvy online and would find out if she continued. He did not want to share her. Fair enough. Did it feel good to get it out in the open like that? Without a doubt, but a couple days later, the fear had settled in. What if he tells someone? She could not bear the thought of that. She could not cope with the repercussions of her family, her close friends, her community finding out. She would be ruined. She would die. They broke up a few months later.[16]

16 At the time of publication, Emily was single and still doing sex work in the province.

"As a female who has done **webcam** work, I fully **support** and agree with sex work as a means of **income**. I was eighteen when I **started** doing it, and did so until around the age of twenty-two. I engaged in this type of activity because I was a **student** at MUN on student loans."

There Is No Such Thing as a Fifteen-Year-Old Prostitute

NICOLE WAS FOURTEEN OR fifteen when she was coerced into prostitution. It wasn't a choice, but it wasn't forced. It was somewhere in between. As an adult she looks back and knows it was abuse. Rape. Slavery.

Nicole left home at an early age and started hanging out with people who were older than her. She ended up at a bar on George Street. At the time, it was a lot easier for underage people to gain entry into bars. She was approached by a tall African-American man.

> He was dressed like a millionaire. He had a nice car. He walked into the bar and it was me and a couple of friends there and he walked up to the bar and looked at me and said, "You've got the most beautiful eyes I've ever seen." I went home with him. That's where it started. It's all he had to say. People think it's this big huge dynamic; it's really not.

A relationship developed, which she believed was honest. He brought her everywhere, paid for everything. They would skip lines to get into clubs. He knew all the important people. If they were at the mall and Nicole wanted something, he got it for her. Then one day he said, "I have no money and my insurance is due." She couldn't do anything about it. She was a teenager without income.

Without saying anything, he brought her to a house on the outskirts of town, told her to go around to the back entrance and do whatever the guy inside asked her to do. Everything changed at that moment. Over the next few years, Nicole was enslaved.

He would tell her that he had friends in law enforcement. There would be times when he would point a gun at her head and let her hear the click as he released the safety. On the day of her little sister's birthday, he drove to her parents' house and told her to go in. When her sister came out, he said she was pretty and he would get her too. These threats were not empty. There were ample visits to the emergency room where nurses could see bruises on her neck and arms. At the time, Nicole wondered why no one was asking questions.

A few years later, the man was brought up on a number of charges. Nicole was part of the case and had to testify about her experience. The medical files were subpoenaed. Notes were inside about possible domestic abuse, but no one took any action, likely because Nicole was over sixteen at the time. If she was younger, it would go directly to Child Youth and Family Services.

The victimization was not solely his doing. There were many men, some his friends, who would do whatever they wanted with Nicole's body and mind. The johns also did whatever they wanted. Nicole mentions the news reports of gang rapes that came out in October 2014.[17]

> It happens all the time. People went right up in arms about it, and I'm thinking, do you really care? There are no services here either. If I was still involved today and I told someone I needed to exit, everybody would have to be fairly creative in order to do that because it's no one's mandate.[18]

17 To read the full CBC article, visit the CBC website.

18 At the time of publication, a new outreach service called Blue Door was just starting in St. John's. Blue Door is funded by the Federal Government and is designed to help women exit the sex industry.

Trying to exit in conjunction with a court case was difficult. Nicole guesses she would have had an easier time if she did it alone.[19] The only gratification was that the guy was sent to prison. "Hearing that guilty verdict was like, *Yes, the judge believed me*." This was such a relief because even some of Nicole's loved ones, who she guesses were embarrassed, cut her out of the family. "They treated me like I was fifty-five when I was just a child."

After the trial, Nicole was referred to therapists to help her deal with her trauma:

> I went to one therapist and she said she couldn't help me because my issues were too complex. She didn't know how to deal with me. I went to another woman. She asked what part did I play in it? Like what do you mean what part did I play in it? I was taking no ownership to any of it, I was a kid.[20] I went a really long time doing drugs, alcohol, not talking to anyone about anything, and I finally got another counsellor. I had been married, separated, all this stuff had happened in my life. I was still miserable. I ended up being referred to someone who finally agreed to treat me, and after a few sessions, he offered me money for sex. This was during our counselling relationship.

Ultimately, this breach cost Nicole every ounce of trust she had. Man or woman—she did not trust anyone.

> There's a lot of shame in that kind of thing because you don't know if everybody's going to understand that this

19 After spending a couple of years volunteering at the Newfoundland and Labrador Sexual Assault Crisis and Prevention Center, I learned that many victims find dealing with the legal system to be the most painful part of the whole experience sometimes. Your past, your motives, your whole life would be opened up for judgment and questioning when you didn't do anything wrong. It would feel like a whole new level of victimization.

20 While it took chutzpah to stand up to her counsellor like this, Nicole was right, and it's mind-boggling to think a counsellor would ask her that question. Where she ended up was not a result of independent adult decision making, at least not on her part. She was a result of immoral actions by others. According to Andre Guindon, in *The Sexual Language: An Essay in Moral Theology*, at her age, Nicole and others in her situation are unable to make decisions for themselves: "The community that trains and educates [children] are responsible for their preparation to become moral agents" (148). Nicole was failed by many around her.

> wasn't a choice you made. You were forced to do it. So
> you go from not wanting to tell anyone anything and
> feeling like you're living a lie or you go full disclosure
> and they disappear because they don't understand or
> they turn out to be the same.

She informed a governing body about this individual's actions, and
the incident was investigated for a number of years. Statements
were taken, but in order for this individual to be charged, Nicole
would have to testify, and she could not stomach having to
sit through another judicial process. She had to back down. "The
system failed me in that situation."

Nicole has worked on her own mental health and wellbeing for years
in order to move past the entrenched anger that has resulted
from all of this. She had a hard time with drugs a number of years
ago because of it. She had lost all hope in people and suffered from
post-traumatic stress disorder (PTSD). Years later she tells her story
to interested organizations and schools, and this engagement
helps her deal with the memories, maintain a healthy confidence,
and provides a cathartic outlet. Talking through her experience over
and over to different audiences helps her gain emotional clarity and
come to terms with why it happened:

> For him to be able to do that to me, I had to be dam-
> aged before I even got to him, because if I was a normal
> fourteen-fifteen year old, for one, I wouldn't be at a
> bar, I would have been at Girl Guides or something.
> Over ninety-five percent of women in the sex trade
> were sexually exploited before they even got there.
> That's a huge number. There's a recipe for it. It just
> doesn't happen randomly to random women. I mean a
> pimp is not going to go after someone who's living at
> home and is happy, who talks to their mom and dad all
> the time, because they're going to go home and say,
> "Mom, this guy did this or said this" and their parents
> will call the cops and the guy will go to jail. So he made

me a recruit. I was young. He's proven to you that he will beat you and line his buddies up for you and all that stuff. It wasn't just empty threats. He never pulled the trigger on the gun, but that's the only thing he didn't do. There's no such thing as a fifteen-year-old prostitute. That needs to just go away. There's no such thing. What difference does it make if a fourteen-year-old girl, their uncle or neighbour or something messes with them, they go to jail. I think it's so much worse when someone's getting money for doing it. People think she ran away from home or she's a hard case, she's troubled. She does drugs. Her family kicked her out. They don't want her. There must be something wrong with her.

That stigma still follows Nicole today, and it used to really upset her. Now she channels those emotions toward being healthy and helping others.

I'm extremely resilient. It's taken twenty years to come out the other end of this. It's the hardest thing. I don't know if anything else has been harder. Nothing. It's not just affected one aspect of your life. It affects everything, and you feel like once you've crossed over that line you can never come back because it's almost like a sense of being ripped off. Like I didn't get to grow up and think the things and do the things that normal kids do. I had all this happen, so it just destroyed all of that, so to be able to get enough strength to want to get past it, sometimes it's just easier to stay in it. I hear a lot of women say, "Well I choose this. I can't get the money this way or that way." I would challenge ninety-eight percent of them. If I'm justifying it, now I'm making my own decision to do it. That doesn't give me strength. I firmly believe that if the numbers tell that over ninety-five percent of women who are into it have been sexually exploited before as a kid, I treat all of it as exploitation. I don't treat any of it as choice. Not everybody agrees with me on that. There's lots of different opinions, but I would challenge some of the people that are trying to stand up for women in the sex trade when they actually have no lived experience or very little education. It has nothing to do with women's rights. I mean that whole system is twisted. I remember saying to myself a few years ago, "This is my choice now. This is my choice to do it. I'm taking my power back." You're not taking anything back if someone's handing you money to use you and abuse you in any way they want. How is that taking power back? It's not. If you asked me ten years ago I'd say this is my choice, of course it is, because I have to say it. If I told you the difference, I'd fall apart. You hold onto it. I firmly believed it at the time, but I was emotionally damaged. You're going to say whatever you have to say so you can be okay in your head.

Part of the outreach work Nicole does aims to educate young women about the dangers of this mindset. The services that we have in St. John's are strengthening, but Nicole thinks there is a lot to do and learn. "I'm a 100 percent believer in harm reduction, but I can't be a part of anything that pumps a woman up to go out on the street. We need a well-tuned machine, people working together. It's good to have people who care, but there's a line."

Most of the outreach and therapy Nicole avails of now is outside of St. John's. She receives rehabilitation for PTSD and has regularly attended a treatment clinic, which she admits has kept her this side of the grave. It was an intense, sixty-day program built to help people with severe anxiety and PTSD. During her last visit, the doctor told her she didn't need to return. "That doesn't mean it's all sunflowers and sunshine. Far from that, but I'm on a much better even keel."

These experiences, all lived before the age of twenty-five, have severely impacted her life. Staying away from drugs and maintaining romantic relationships have been struggles, but after all the challenges, Nicole identifies not as a victim but a survivor. Perhaps this survival mentality has been inside her since childhood. How else could she find the strength to testify, go through the process of attempting to bring a corrupt counsellor to justice, and open herself to the public by giving talks and reliving the worst parts of her life for educational purposes? To most women, what she's lived through, what's she's survived, is the stuff of nightmares.[21]

---

21 The Coalition Against the Sexual Exploitation of Youth (CASEY) released a report on sexual exploitation in the province in 2011, which was quashed by the provincial government until 2015. You can read the full report here:
http://www.exec.gov.nl.ca/exec/wpo/publications/STR.pdf

" Guys are getting off work, and I know it sounds really gross, but they want to hook up before they go home to their families, or they'll leave half an hour early in the morning and they'll come see us before they go to work. **"**

I Feel Like Mrs. Anybody

AFTER THE CAR ACCIDENT, she lost her car as well as her license. She became reliant on her sister to get to work at the pharmaceutical factory, but her sister was just about to quit. They were sitting in the cafeteria on their lunch break, the smell of toast and cigarette smoke wafting around them, and she saw an ad that promised $1000 a week for dancing. She slipped off her hairnet and threw it down on the table, looked at her sister, who had stripped once or twice before. *Faisons-le.* "Let's do it."

She was scared. She wasn't certain. But for damn sure she was excited.

In Montreal, dancing was a normal thing. "The French didn't look down on you the way people do in Newfoundland, so it wasn't a big deal to try it." She was eighteen. She couldn't look men in the eye. She was wearing $5 shoes and a $5 bikini. Couldn't dance. Would just stare at the other women. They seemed like a different species. It took a lot for her to get up on that stage in those heels, but she did it. It was like she was born in those heels. That was ten years ago.

She heard rumours from other dancers that you could make ten grand a week in Newfoundland. A self-proclaimed hustler at the time, she couldn't turn that money down. So she saved up $800, which was a lot for her then, and came here.

It was her first time on a plane. She had no idea where in the world she was going. But when she arrived, she was dropped off at the club, given a key to the dancers' house, and started working right away.[22] She thought the club was beautiful. Classy. A step above almost every other club she'd experienced.

Some dancers do not consider stripping sex work, but Brook does.[23] "It's definitely sex industry. People touching your naked body, selling yourself, your body, and it's sexual when you're dancing for a customer. There's money exchanged."

Once in a while, she admits, a guy will offer a large sum of money, sometimes to the tune of $1000 for a night with a dancer. Brook has experience high-end escorting, charging no less than $500 a session. She took breaks while in relationships as she draws the line at having sex for money while romantically involved.

Though she has dabbled in that lifestyle, she has managed to block it out because "it fucks you up." Brook says it can cause problems when you're having sex for fun and then for money. Lines can be blurred. It can mess with your sex life in unsettling ways. She admits that in some situations she felt more at ease with customers than with her romantic partners. She acknowledges a thought many women feel, that when you're with someone for so long, there's pressure to step up your game, bring something new, keep it interesting. The new comfort could stem from the fact that they're paying $500 to $1000. They obviously think she's worth it.

> I don't hide my fat. I don't worry about the position I'm in wondering is my fat showing, or am I doing a good job. What is he going to think? I didn't care. It was just a free for all. I was liberated. I love sex. I love sex. Making money and sex for me is like one beside the other, you know what I mean?

---

22 The dancer's house is owned by the club and available to come-from-away workers.

23 At one point I was contacted by an anonymous dancer from the mainland who pointed me to some useful articles about the nature of dancing as art and not sex work. It's important to note this alternative perspective since, for many people, stripping is not considered sex work.

She loves playing that role, even though sometimes it can be tiring. Fifty percent of the time, she finds it pleasurable. There has only been one instance in her life where she felt victimized, and it was because the customer did not pay her. She blames herself for that, having learned to get the cash up front. "What are you going to do against a man? I'm not going to call the cops. I'm not going to fight you. You're an asshole. It's hard. You feel almost raped when that happens, but it's not the same thing."[24] The first time she escorted, she was eighteen and was paid $240 for a night. She thought she was rich. Currently, she does not advertise for escort work and says she would never advertise on websites. If it comes to her, she considers it, but her main work is dancing.

The "Englishmen" here in Newfoundland are nice compared to the French, who she describes as arrogant and cheap. She plans to stay here to finish her career, "If you can call it a career," she said.

> I'm here nine months of the year and I work every day. I'm a workaholic. I love my job, but I'm the type of person that gets stressed easily. I'm anxious. When I cross those doors, though, everything falls away. I just concentrate on my job. I have a few drinks. More than a few. I'm a drinker.

Brook doesn't do drugs, at least not on a regular basis. Once in a while she'll take something, but at work, it's purely drinking:

> I just take a few drinks and all my troubles go away. All the stress goes away. I love it. I love talking to people. I'm not one of those dancers that will go with a customer and be cold and robotic about it. I treat customers with respect. I listen to them. I say, "Hi, how are you." They love my company. They know I'm not fake doing it. This is my life. This is what I do.

Some girls consider it work, but Brook considers it a lifestyle. "I feel good. I look good. I love it."

---

24 Brook went on to repeat that she knows it's not the same thing, but similar because there's a power shift and someone is being exploited.

When men go to the strip club it's usually to party and to spend money, and Brook enjoys the benefits. In Montreal, the massage parlours, especially, offer sex work and it's comparatively cheap. Brook says it was hard to make any money just by dancing. She recalls that it was $60 for a sensual massage. The men would prefer to spend their money there, but Newfoundlanders, she says, like spending money on curvy girls. "I'm not skinny. Montreal, they like skinny, skinny. Here they prefer curvy, so I do really good here compared to a lot of other girls, but the fact that I love my job helps too. They're kind and respectful in general." Generally. Brook is quick to point out that there's a raw reality to the job. "We're not working in a church. You have those guys that come and disrespect you, but we have our bouncers and they got our backs."

She was quick to express disappointment in some other dancers who overcharge and are dishonest with the customer.[25] Many of the women overcharge. They will continue the lap dance unbeknownst to the customer that for every three minutes an extra $20 is being added to their bill. Brook prefers to keep it straight.[26]

She just wants to do her job and if anyone interferes in that, she takes issue. A lot of the girls, she says, run in packs, but she's a loner, prefers to do her own thing. You can't trust everyone. "They'll say hi to your face but stab you in the back." Every two to three months, she'll go out to a nice dinner at The Keg or some other downtown restaurant with some of the other girls, but rarely:

> I don't need friends. I got my work and me. I like men.
> I get along with men. I feel like men are more real
> sometimes than women. I know how to talk with them.
> I know how to deal with them. A lot of dancers like
> other women. I'm not into women. Maybe after twenty
> of those [points to her peach-coloured cocktail on the
> table] maybe for money. Like upstairs we do lesbian

25 I was talking to one male friend who went to the Cotton Club and ended up getting a lap dance. After the lap dance, the dancer said he owed triple what he agreed to pay. She got mad and the bouncer got involved. The guy had to leave the bar even though he felt he didn't do anything wrong.

26 All the dancers I've spoken to as well as one strip-club worker said the competition and cattiness amongst the dancers is one of the hardest things to deal with in this environment.

shows and there's one girl here that I used to do time with. I liked it. It was okay, but some girls just like women and I'm like, no, I want men.

When she brings a man upstairs to the lap-dance area, she respects them because if she steals she knows they won't come back.

> You're stealing from the club? It's like my home. It's like you're stealing from my home. They don't respect. There's no respect. It's kinda like in the drug world. There's territories. There's respect. It's like a game. It's the same thing. You don't charge less. You respect. They steal all the time and it takes money out of my pocket. You don't go see that customer while I'm talking to them. In Montreal, if you do that, you're getting your ass beat. Here? No one wants to lose their job so we stay more quiet. I'm not a fighter. I hate fighting. I'm a lover, but sometimes you can't take it. I don't cause trouble. I don't fight. I sell liquor. I do my thing.

Brook's thing is trying to keep the money flowing. While some of the girls have regulars, she doesn't. She prefers new men because it's exciting. "Dancing for the same person, it gets heavy, you know what I mean? What do I do next? He saw everything."

Brook doesn't have a man in her life right now. A personal relationship just ended, so she may have to move. The dancer's house was her home when she first moved to Newfoundland, then she rented a condo, but that option is too expensive now. One never knows what kind of money can be made, or not, in a week's work.[27] Brook says she can be broke one night and have $600 in her pocket the next. Regardless of the insecure payment schedule, Brook is in it for the attention.

> I love the attention, of course. The men, every day I hear, "Wow, you're so gorgeous, you're so gorgeous." It

---

[27] To give it some perspective, according to *Sex at Dawn: How We Mate, Why We Stray, and What It Means for Modern Relationships* by Christopher Ryan and Cecilia Jethá, "Americans spend more money at strip clubs than at Broadway, off-Broadway, regional and nonprofit theaters, the opera, the ballet and jazz and classical music performances—combined" (3).

makes you feel good about yourself. I feel so sexy when I'm working. I feel like Mrs. Anybody. I'm so short. I'm a little chunky. I put my heels on, I'm taller. I put my make-up on. My hair done. I feel good about myself. It's positivity.

Sitting on the bar stool in her black-satin robe and a black bra and underwear set, she has no problem showing me parts of her body during this conversation. Her body looks natural to me with the exception of her bleached blond hair, but she has had $30,000 worth of plastic surgery. She's had her butt done twice, liposuction once, her breasts augmented, and she gets her lips done every seven months. The buttock surgery includes taking fat out of places where you don't want it, such as your stomach, and then implanting it in your buttock to make it look full. "I love fat," said Brook. "I put the fat in the bum for the Brazilian bum situation."

The lips are injected with Juvéderm. She once had small lips and now they are full and plump even though she said she's due for an injection. Other than lip injections, Brook's next surgery will cost $11,000. "My bum cost me $15,000 so far, so my bum is going to be worth $26,000 soon. I'm stopping after that. I have this picture of my body in my head that I want. I'm twenty-eight. When I'm thirty it will be exactly how I want it. Big bums are so famous now." We joke that Kim Kardashian made the big butt famous.

She has four tattoos, all with their own symbolism. She shows me a loony-size tattoo of a shark on her tiny wrist. The girls that hustle— the ones that make the most money—are called sharks. She has one of a dancer with fistfuls of money falling down around her, a kind of self-image. She has a broken-heart tattoo that symbolizes her own heart, broken over and over again. She flips through her phone to retrieve an image of her next tattoo, which represents the men in her life that are dead to her.[28] Ghosts in her memory. "They pulled me down a lot of my life. I've dated a lot of bad men, but I like bad boys. I can't help it."

---

28 By request, the description of that tattoo has been omitted.

The bad boys come and go in Brook's life, but the only real negative she sees in her life is the alcohol consumption. She feels like she's killing herself.

> I drink seven days a week, sometimes for 100 days in a row. No one does that. And I drink hard liquor. I drink cognac, so I'm always scared that I'm not going to pass thirty-five years old doing that. I drink about twenty ounces of alcohol every day, which is twenty shots. I want to make it to at least fifty. I want to live. I love life. I want kids. I want to see them grow up. I stress about these things.

She takes a sip of her drink. The heavy clunk of platform heels around us echo from the wooden floor.

When she's not drunk she makes more money. She's clear. Remembers who she was and wasn't speaking to, remembers where conversations were left. She's more focused. Her pattern is to cure her hangover with another night of drinking. The hangover and the drinking make everything hard on the body, but it makes everything easier on the mind. She admits that nearly every woman she works with has either a drug problem or a drinking problem or both. This is a stereotype that exists for a reason. The upside is she sells a lot of alcohol for the club.

Although the alcohol is a problem, she feels that nothing can bring her down. She considers herself a real hustler. Works as much as possible, is hard on herself for missing time. If she takes one day off, she loses sleep over it. She used to be the type of girl that was super shy, afraid to speak her mind. Now, she considers herself a strong woman; if someone tries to manipulate her, she stands up for herself. She doesn't let anyone take advantage of her, and she's proud and happy about how strong she has become. Everything she does, she does of her own free will.

Most of Brook's family and friends know what she does for a living. Her mother said she wasn't surprised and was okay with it. Her father, someone who hasn't been in her life on a regular basis, didn't say much about it, but was happy that she was making money. "I was very independent. My own person. My parents were friends more than parents, like I brought myself up. Kind of. They had nothing to say. I do what I do." She dismisses the friends she's lost along the way as being a natural part of life and growing up. Not everyone can stay in touch. Her sister is still a big part of her life. She reminisces about some times her and her sister shared earlier in their lives, but says she can't remember much. If so, "I would be insane." Brook laughed and picked up her drink. She plans to dance as long as she can.

"The **hardest** thing about this job is maintaining my **bikini wax.**"

Make it Clean Through Creative Work

MEGAN AND I MET at the downtown Piatto location on a humid summer evening. We opted for a table outside away from the heat and close seating arrangement. Since finishing her graduate degree, sex-based service work and some other side jobs have allowed her to keep a roof over her head and invest in her own business. Her service, which she's been doing for six years, stands apart from many others around town. She specializes in touch, which is a bit difficult to wrap your head around until you hear it explained. It's a kind of sex work that is not as blatant or as literal as intercourse or oral sex. It's more sophisticated. It combines aspects of pressure points and erogenous zones; it's part massage, part sexual pleasure, part tantric, part spiritual.

Megan doesn't dress the way you might think. She wears jeans and a T-shirt. No make-up. Just clean and natural. Her hair is cut short and she has an athletic build. The clients typically feel at ease around her. "They see someone like me and think that's more comfortable for them. It's who I am. I'm not trying to make any particular thing work for me. It's just who I am. The rest is too much work. I don't have that kind of time or interest in putting that kind of effort in."

First when she started doing sex work she would do outcalls to downtown hotels, which was risky. Later, she networked with other service providers and they shared a space similar to a timeshare where they would book their time in a calendar and certain people would get certain days. Having control over the space is a comfort. "You have the ball in your court a little bit more. They don't know what's behind the door. There could be somebody else in the place for all they know. They just don't know. It shifts the dynamic for sure." The place she uses now is discreet and safe. The downstairs neighbours might have some inkling, but they stay out of it.

She vets the clients through an email exchange during which she gauges their personality from the way they correspond. She considers not just their writing style but what they actually say, how much they divulge, how sincere they seem. They tell her things about themselves, and she asks questions. While there's no face-to-face exchange, there is some honesty. Through this process, she slowly disarms.

While most clients are good and exactly what you'd expect, there are some memorable ones. One client's body was the texture of wood. He was so tense. She suspects this was a manifestation of his mental state and that he probably had something on his mind. Another client expressed his love for her. Another started stalking her, found her at her regular place of work, and really could have caused a lot of upheaval in her life. The situation was brought under control without too much disturbance. While some clients cross lines, most are normal and receptive to the experience. Some have been dealing with serious personal or physical challenges. One had a partner who was terminally ill and they had not been physically cared for in years. Another had bad psoriasis. She did not turn them away as others might. It's not about her, she says. Essentially she is there to provide a service. Most of her clients are regulars, and they pay top dollar. While the majority are men, there are some couples. When servicing couples, she will sometimes excuse herself so they can be alone. The couples are usually looking for her to teach them how to engage each other in more intimate ways. She considers this a gift.

Megan appreciates that her work simply makes people really happy. They then take that happiness and contentment out into the world with them. During each session, there is a continuous flow of communication in order to engage the body in the right way, but it's about more than that. Some have their own anxieties about the whole experience; they are unsure what to expect or become scared about how this interaction or discovery makes them feel.

> My favourite thing is when I touch them somewhere and they say, "What the fuck was that?" and we laugh. The client recognizes more of their potential, whatever that is. Ultimately it's healthy for them when they bring it back to their regular lives. It's like I'm facilitating the connection they have to themselves and to something larger than themselves. It's an experience that includes the body but is not solely about the body. Some clients are open to the spiritual conversation, and I'm intro-ducing them to that component through the physical body.

Because of the multifaceted objective of the session, it is neither rushed nor timed. It's not about the sexual gratification, but about the holistic experience. Intimacy becomes a huge part of it. A philo-sophical conversation can form, spiritual connections can be made. "I never think of it as sex work, for the record." It's more than that.

Out of all the interviews I conducted, Megan's stance on sex work's relationship to feminism was the most nuanced. She stepped into it from a place of knowledge, from knowing others in the business.

> It was a source of possibility and potential from a financial perspective and also being independent, having control over one's work schedule. I put myself through school, and more school. So I have debt, but the best part is paying more of that off. This will help me. But you know, what I thought would be a seven-year plan to do the schooling and then get this other thing going, which was three to four years from conception to capital to starting the program, it took me two-and-a-half years. That's not how I initially

thought it was going to go. Yet, I still see that this form of work is traditional. It's the type of work that is mostly provided by women, for men who have money. And the men who have money, they have their money, you know, from the stock market, from those who inherited family business, natural resources, so I see that I'm a part of a larger system that's not changing at all. I'm also just one part in it. I actually had this conversation a couple of years ago with some people who are in fine arts in Alberta. All of their funding comes from oil and natural resources in a way. They get to produce this piece of work and the money is already dirty. They sort of saw it as like money laundering. Here, take this money that's dirty and make it clean through creative work. So at some level I see it being like, okay, yes I'm playing a part and am somewhat complicit in this structure, but how can I take the resources that come through this and launder them into being essentially something good? My schooling and training is also service based and for people's good. For me, all of the work I do is just all around the same thing; it's just slightly different. I'm not like, "This is super empowering." Empowerment would suggest one didn't have any power before and that's not true. It just depends on how you want to understand the type of power. Most people come to understand that there is an exchange that happens. You're giving suggestions that are asking them to open up their senses to notice what they're hearing, smelling, seeing, maybe the weight of their own body, what they're feeling. You have people just continually entering into that moment, into sensations in their body. And not only just sensations, but usually really pleasant sensations, where they're like, "This feels good," and you're like, "Keep noticing how that feels, keep noticing what feeling good feels like, and just keep entering into that." People just drop into a trancelike kind of a place. You could say they drop into a level of awareness and consciousness that tends to be almost like being asleep, but it's pleasure, and it's so different from their normal reality. Arguably, it's more real than what they're used to. So then they're just like, "I don't know what the fuck that was." Men will say they feel like they just orgasmed but didn't ejaculate. They think it's impossible.

This is not something that can be reproduced each time. It depends on why they're there. Some are interested in the process. Some keep returning because they're getting something more out of it.

It's helping open up their perspective that there's something besides their reality. There's also ritual, maybe even a historical retrospective; regardless, someone comes for healing, there's an offering. There is a monetary exchange because we're such a money-based country, people think money symbolizes power. It symbolizes something. Not just power. I come from privilege. I'm okay looking, white, I kind of understand I have a certain amount of savvy, and I can just see that allows me to do this a little bit easier. I'm doing the path that I was put here to do. We are not separate entities.

After speaking to Megan for a few hours, I got the sense that she was very at peace. I actually could feel that peacefulness, that mindfulness and clarity, coming from her. It in turn made me feel peaceful. When I expressed that, she said that's exactly part of her path. She knows that one of her purposes in life is to provide service to better the lives of others.

"**Rape** is something you learn to **walk away** from."

Every Single Penny

THE COTTON CLUB IS the oldest and most popular strip club in St. John's. They have about twenty-five people on payroll and between twenty-five to thirty dancers, depending on the season. Beer costs $7 and cover is $10. The people who usually go there have money to spend. They have a lot of regulars, tourists, and business people arriving from major cities. "Business men, when they're away from home, go to the strip club. That's what they do," says Jacquie, a bartender and manager.

Jacquie has been a spectator at the Cotton Club for a long time. She has tended bar for almost a decade and has seen it all. She's never danced, but because of her long hair, slim build, and large breasts, many patrons have thought otherwise.

Jacquie has seen it all while working bar and claims she has "bajillions of stories" about men and sex:

> They're just so weak. They have no self-control when it comes to sex. Especially after a few drinks, and once they're up over those stairs, they change. They definitely do. I've had guys down here and they're sweet as pie. So nice. They'll throw a compliment here or there. I've had guys upstairs be like, "I'd love to titty fuck the shit out of you" or "Holy shit, missus, look at the tits on ya" or "Your ass looks great in that," and I'd be like, "Would you like a Blue Star, sir? This is a public place."

> I just brush it off, but it gets to the point where if I
> feel uncomfortable I'll tell them right off.

They assume that because she works in a strip club, and she wears low-cut tops, like most bartenders and waitresses in other restaurants and bars, that she is easy and that they can say whatever comes to mind.

She chalks it up to the fact that they're bombarded by naked women. They're drunk. Turned on. She's never had anyone say anything remotely as graphic while working in a regular bar situation. "As soon as we go up over those stairs…it's wild. It blows my mind. I'm like you're a sweet old man and now I just look at you like you're a dirty perv like the rest of them. It's true. It's unfortunate."

While Jacquie has never been overtly threatened, she has had experiences where the guys just seem like creeps. They stand by the bar, say something obscene. They are completely annihilated. They might be flirting, but it comes across as pure nastiness. If Jacquie isn't too offended or annoyed by it, she plays along. When it becomes too much, she walks away.

"I'd say it's happened about half a dozen times where I've felt like, okay, this guy needs to go. He could have waited for me after work. If he's like, 'Oh I'm not here for them, I'm here for you,' I'm like, 'Oh yeah, you paid $10 cover and $7 a beer to come talk to a bartender. Fat chance, buddy.'"

Like most bars, no one leaves alone at the end of the night. Everyone makes sure people get in cabs or one of the bouncers will walk the girls to their cars.

> There are sex-crazed lunatics out there. They could just
> be waiting out there having a smoke and we're leaving
> thirty minutes afterwards. I've never felt like actually
> something would happen in this building, but after
> the fact, sure. Guys that were really aggressive with
> their approach, I'd think, I bet he's the type of guy

that would wait for you outside or overheard me say, "Oh I'm going to the afterhours tonight," and he'd show up there.

While the customers can sometimes cross lines, so too can the dancers. There are certain things dancers are not allowed to do at the club, such as have sex with the patrons. While it's a full-contact bar, which means customers can touch the dancers during lap dances within reason, there are some rules the dancers are supposed to follow. Some of the girls are on the adult-service sites advertising that they're dancing at the club in the nighttime and meeting up with clients there. "We do not solicit here. We are a full-contact dance bar, but we do not sell sex in any way."

Patrons and dancers alike sometimes forget that there are sixteen cameras located throughout the building, most of them upstairs. Fines have been doled out to dancers. If they offer sex services outside the normal, they get a second chance, but then they're asked to leave because it gives the bar a bad name. "It's not worth it for us. Our business is alcohol and entertainment. We're not here to sell sex. What happens after the fact has nothing to do with us."

In the club, the game is all about getting lap dances because that's the only real way a dancer can make bank. The dancers are not on payroll at the bar. They are booked almost like short-term contract workers. Whatever money they make on their lap dances is theirs to keep as well as what they make in tips on stage. And they work hard for their tips. Many of the girls are hustlers in that they will do whatever they need to do to make more money. There have been incidents in the past where dancers have tried to steal from customers, and they have been swift to correct it, maintaining a zero-tolerance policy for that kind of behavior. If a dancer does that once, she's fired.

> We had this one girl, about two months ago, guy came in, hardworking guy, works like two jobs. We know him really well. His phone went missing, and it wasn't

his personal phone. It was his company phone, so he was really upset. He was really upset because he was like all of his contacts were gone: he travelled for work, all his meetings were saved in his phone. He was really distraught. He never mentioned that he took a girl home after, took her back to his house and whatever. He claimed they just hung out and had a few drinks, but she actually stole his phone, and we went to the dancer house and called his phone, she didn't even turn it off—idiot—and it rang. We found his phone and he was so grateful.

They fired the dancer on the spot.

"They even rob from each other. We have lockers with locks on them, but girls drink while they're working, put their purses down for a second, and it's gone. Everything is so much drama because it's all about the money."

For the club, it's about getting a good balance of dancers—you can't have everyone look the same. There needs to be diversity. At the time of the interview, Jacquie said there were a lot of African-American girls, so in order to earn a place on the roster as another African American, a woman had to be physically immaculate. "It's not going to work with this demographic here in Newfoundland. It's not. Maybe in Ontario or Montreal. We need at least fifty-fifty." Sometimes Jacquie has to get honest with the girls. If they keep calling looking for work, sometimes she will come out and say, 'Listen, you need to lose ten pounds before you get on stage again. Go to the gym for the next month, give me a call and one-hundred percent.' One woman did exactly that and returned to dancing a month later. This was after spending a few months doing sex work with another woman and finding that it did not suit her.

It is a transient business for the dancers. They come and go out of the club and the lifestyle. The men rarely change in that every type of man, from all demographics, visits the Cotton Club, and of course, there's the odd stag party prowling through. "I'm gonna say that we have youngsters, like nineteen, all the way up to sixty, seventy-year-old men. There's no specific clientele. It's a good mixture. On Friday and Saturday nights you're going to get all the youngsters and whatnot, throughout the week it's predominately older men."

They used to have a rule that women were not allowed to enter the club without a male, but they eliminated that regulation to welcome members of the lesbian population.

> Our Tuesday night is free ladies night. We do get a lot more women then. We get women who come here just because their guy friends want them to come here. I don't think it's genuinely that they want to come here and see the show. Most of them are here just ripping the dancers apart. You get up there and do it then if you're so…you might have a hotter body, but you don't have the confidence to get up there in front of a room full of people. They say it right in front of [the dancers] too. They're just instigating the situation. So we don't get very many women. It's something we're trying to push, but women don't spend as much money as men, so I'm not putting too much emphasis on it. It would be nice.

The rule used to exist to stop women from entering the club and catching their partners participating in or witnessing some lewd act. It doesn't happen often, but sometimes women will show up looking for their husbands or boyfriends and might end up dragging them out the door, which always arouses hollers and laughs from the other patrons.

One night a dancer asked to leave early. Something had come up, and she could not fulfill her nightly time on stage. She wasn't supposed to leave, but she got word that her father was coming down to the bar as part of a bachelor party. She could not vacate the premises fast enough.

The bouncers are the ones who see it all. They expel multiple people from the premises every night mostly because the patrons get too drunk. If a guy gets caught upstairs doing something inappropriate, it's automatic dismissal. Also, the men are not allowed to touch the dancers while they're on the floor or stage. Upstairs only.

The only time those rules don't apply is if a heterosexual or same-sex couple goes upstairs for a lap dance. The dancers can use their discretion.

> There's certain things that are 100 percent no, but some girls won't let certain things happen. Guys feel like they got gypped at some points. They're like, "She never got naked." And I'm like, "Some girls won't take their panties off." Like they'll take their tops off but not their panties unless it's like five or six songs in, but for them to go up there for three minutes for twenty dollars, they're not getting fully nude, and I completely understand that. Know what I mean? So when I hear complaints about that, I brush it off. If a guy was up there for ten or twelve songs and she still never took her panties off, I'd be like, he could have went with someone else that would have. I mean they're not allowed to touch any southern areas so that shouldn't be the issue, but for the visual stimulation—he's spending two to three hundred bucks.

From a managerial standpoint, one of the hardest things to deal with is the dancer drama. They don't get along in the house. They can't dance together. They get into fights. Not everyone is like this, but enough to make it a thing. The club has also stopped collecting money for the girls after lap dances because some of them were overcharging, ultimately robbing the customers. If drunk, a man doesn't typically remember how many songs have passed while a mostly naked woman is gyrating on top of him with her breasts in his face.

Girls just get aggressive, assaulting customers, taking their shoes off, like beating them with their shoes. We had this one guy who had a shoe impaled in his head and the ambulance was called and everything. He was going to press charges and everything, and the girl left that night, went right to the airport and left. But sometimes for the sake of sixty bucks, if you think about it, what they're doing for that money, I'd want every single penny too.

"They look down on us, feel we were asking for trouble or may even deserve it."

Hoops

HANNAH IS A THIRTY-SOMETHING professional who has a lucrative daytime job, grew up in a small town in Newfoundland, has family and contacts all over the province, from Central to the West and South coasts, had the most normal upbringing she can imagine, has neither been the victim of any crime nor suffered any physical or sexual abuse. She is highly educated, has held respected research positions in her field, has a graduate degree, and works in medicine. She moved to St. John's in her twenties to attend university.

She chose to explore the service-provider role to supplement funding for her education without having to take student loans. It was a way to increase her quality of life and not incur debt.

> I don't want to make the generalization that all the other service providers are in a situation of desperation. Some are single parents or don't have an education or any option, so there is sort of a different level of desperation or need that I have never felt, so I have never felt like a victim in that way. It wasn't out of desperation.

She knew exactly what she was getting into. If anything, she educated herself on what to look for and the ways of protecting herself. Around the time of our interview, there were a few news pieces about local outbreaks of syphilis. Hannah is adamant about taking precautions to limit the amount of risk she is confronting and is very upfront with clients, ninety percent of which are returning. She wears condoms every time for everything. No condom: No sex. "I make it a policy to get tested at least every six months, and I have absolutely zero history of any STD or STI as a result of my very, very staunch nature on that. It's a risky industry and people need to be gently reminded that what you do can have a lifelong consequence."

Because of the health risks associated with this lifestyle, there are certain things she won't do, and there is a filtering process that occurs before any sexual activity happens. She has strict rules that she follows every time until she knows who she's dealing with. She stresses cleanliness and respect. Age doesn't matter. Physical appearance or level of fitness is beside the point. What matters is if they're polite and willing to respect the fact that it's safe services or no services. As a rule she will not perform any kind of full service on a first meeting.

"I know that the gentlemen who are willing to go through these hoops are obviously reasonable people, so I feel a little less insecure about meeting them for the first time; in fact, I have such a great rapport with some of them I actually feel like I'm on a real date with some of them. We'll actually sit down and have a glass of wine and chat about our week."[29]

HANNAH'S CLIENTS TRUST HER implicitly to the point where some use their real names and divulge information about their private lives. She has seen some in her place of work. "I've crossed paths with them. I have not even looked at them or given them away. I am very in tune with the fact that I have to respect their privacy, and like I said, I have just as much to lose as they do. I'm in a career besides this."

They see that she's legitimate, the pictures she gives them before the meeting are actually her, they pay their agreed upon price, they do

---

29 Hearing that the role of service provider is also that of confidant is not new. Many women in the industry have echoed this experience.

not try to manipulate or surprise her. They know it is worth the concession to get clean, reasonable service. She usually offers foreplay, oral sex, and what most of her clients seem to want, which is foot worship. That is the most Hannah will provide on a first meeting. She may offer intercourse or anal sex to some clients based on her impression of them and if they tend to be trustworthy. She doesn't play to fetishes other than foot. "I have one guy who wanted to have extremely rough sex and wanted choking involved. I said, 'You know I respect the fact that's what you're interested in. I don't have the trust there. It's not you personally. Good luck.'"

Because Hannah is in her thirties, her clients are typically forty to sixty years of age, some blue-collar workers and some white-collar workers, business men who are probably making six figures with the first figure not being a one, she says. Most are men who don't like the idea of having to go to a hotel. She lives in a secure building where she can buzz people in, there's off-street parking, people come and go all the time. So there's no awkward walk through a hotel lobby or the worry that you may run into someone you know. Plus there's extra security in the apartment building. If anything ever happened to Hannah, she could just scream and people would hear her. She has done a few out calls with regulars, but she never proposes that possibility because clients are pursuing it on a second or third meet, and she certainly is not willing to do that. She likes the sense of control, but not in a dominating way, in a way that is conducive to safety and security.

Part of that safety and security is keeping this part of her life secret. No one in her professional or personal life is aware of her secondary means of income:

> There are a few girls, local providers, who I have sort of struck up a rapport with, but it's a conversation via email where we email each other potential aliases to look out for and why. We exchange stories and whatnot. We can vent that way, but no one in my

family. People in my personal life would be shocked. I'm always the good girl. Always the academically inclined, you know.

She admits though that she's not the conservative person a lot of people think she is or once believed herself to be.

> People are often perplexed just by how open-minded and how non-judgmental I am about things like transgenderism and fetishes as long as it's done in a respectful, non-vulgar manner. They very rarely get a rise out of me, like it's very hard to shock me, and I never thought I'd be able to say that about the sex industry…Unless you are actually in the industry you sort of have these preconceptions based on what the media shapes on the news of the prostitute— that's the common terminology on the American news stories—assaulted in a hotel room or a street worker overdosed on cocaine in Detroit. I mean, they don't think about people who are highly hygienic or educated or articulate, the very cautious, diligent people. It just doesn't go with the stereotype so you have to fight against that. You know the first thing people would say is, "Why? You have so many options, why?" It's kind of hard to give them an answer that would really make them understand.

For Hannah, the perspective is likened to the way some people view sexuality. Some people will not be labelled and they like the company of more than one gender, but they may be married with children and a wife. "Some people say you're either gay or straight, you're either good or bad. Whatever it is. I find that the views on that are similar to the views on gender roles and sexuality. Certainly here in this province anyway."

So why would Hannah do it? What's the payoff besides extra cash for someone who is independent, has an advanced education and a highly respectable career?

Initially there was some elation that somebody was willing to pay me to be with me when friends of mine were
sort of complaining that there are no good men around,
nothing. So there was sort of a psychological fulfillment
initially, but I've surpassed that now. It's really not
about ego gratification at all. I'm certainly not an ego-
maniac but there was that titillation and curiousness
and everything else so there was a little bit of a psychological fulfillment for me, but at the same time, as
you already know, it was just a quick and easy way to
catch up or even get ahead when I finished school or
even work around my schedule. I was almost my own
boss or an entrepreneur running the business the way
I saw fit without having to build the business from the
ground up if that makes sense.

Her clients are always surprised that she has a graduate level of
education and a good, full-time public job, which speaks to the
fact that it's outside the norm for sex workers. Sometimes they are
intimidated by it.

There's a lot of men out there whether they're willing to
admit it or not or whether they're self-aware of it or
not. They could probably go out and find an attractive
woman for a sort of no-strings-attached-friends-with-
benefits arrangement but there's some sort of pleasure
they get from the perceived dominance of paying for
it, like somebody's serving you and you need to do what
they want, and I guess somebody in my position who
is very picky about who she meets and under what kind
of circumstances or what kind of services initially,
knowing that this doesn't pay my bills, it keeps me at a
certain level of lifestyle and is helping me to save for
that down payment, etc., on a condo or a house. It
takes the strong hold or power away from them. Men
who are not wanting control in the bedroom are quite

comfortable and find it endearing. Men who are very, very dominant find it very threatening. That's just my perception of it whether it's vocalized or not. It's very obvious in some people and it's less of an issue now because the people who are comfortable with me, and know what I'm all about and know that I'm harmless, come back because it doesn't surprise them or bother them or intimidate them anymore.

Some of Hannah's regulars have been with her for two years. They share a mutually beneficial relationship that has no strings attached. The clients were seeking one person who would fit their needs, mesh with their personality, and who had a respectful standard for themselves. Frankly, she was surprised by the amount of men who were looking for this type of relationship, one that is long term and comfortable but without emotional commitment.

The dominant stress of being a service professional is, for Hannah, the stress of getting to know someone and gaining a suspicion that they are not who they say they are. The paranoia can creep in. "I have to say I have been very fortunate in that most of my negative experiences have been in that initial screening process where I have had to politely and respectfully tell men that I don't think our interests are aligned and that I'm not the service provider for them. A few of them have not taken that well and they have made life a little bit of a living hell for me at times."

One man in particular posted Hannah's pictures without her consent. She sends pictures out to clients sometimes. Her face is never shown. Any tattoos she may have are Photoshopped out. She has had to work with the administrator of the adult-advertising site to get to the bottom of it. "They were blocked for posting my pictures without expressed written consent, which is in violation of a cyber-bully act and technically a criminal offence." In another incident, one guy propositioned her for a threesome with him and his girlfriend and the picture he sent was of Hannah herself. Another gentlemen told her he was forty and then admitted to being sixty-eight before the meeting.

A browse through the local adult-classifieds site reveals a whole range of posts, some are regular posts by people just looking for some fun, and there are others who are looking for public sex and very specific fetishes. "It really surprises me how many unwell individuals are on that site where a whole host of aliases—literally there are, even just a few that I know—have ten to twelve different aliases or accounts on that site and that's what they do, they go in and try to play games with different girls, and they'll post a lot of false information. I feel sorry for the legitimate clients."[30]

The prevalence of these questionable posts and people adds to the worry that Hannah could meet an unbalanced person. For Hannah, it has opened her mind to the fact that first impressions can often be misleading when they're made during online interactions since tone and other verbal cues are unavailable. Hannah will engage someone on the phone first before meeting them.

> People come across as quite quirky. Maybe it's that they don't have the vocal communication or the ability to communicate effectively through the written word and I find them to be the sweetest people when I talk to them on the phone and also when I meet them. I have no problem, and that's someone that I would initially have written off.

Conversely, some people are quite charming online, and when she meets them in person, she quickly realizes she wants nothing to do with them.

Boundary pushers are the ones Hannah stays away from—the ones that enjoy pushing her buttons.

> They will tell you they want one thing and that certain things are okay and they respect this and respect that, and when they get there in person, they think the rules are going to change. Because I'm so up front about who

---

30 Part way through my research there was someone who posted on the site that I was a scam—not a woman looking to interview sex workers for a book, but a man who was getting off on acting like one.

I am and what I'm all about, I don't have any patience or respect for that, so that's basically what I've learned. That is that even though this technological age has opened up a chance for someone to be a service provider who would never have considered it before, it has opened it up in a way that also sort of eliminates the human contact, and you're really left with having to rely on sort of a gut feeling sometimes. Sometimes you're wrong.

Hannah recounts one story that stands out in her mind and speaks to that experience:

He was the sweetest man. There was nothing violent or threatening about him. He was five foot three—he probably weighed less than me, I wasn't in fear for my safety in any means—educated, well-spoken man. I made it very clear to him, and we had met twice before and he said, "I'd really like full service Friday night. Some wine, some conversation and make it a full night, you and me. No other clients." That's not a problem. I didn't know anything before he was trying to penetrate me without putting on a condom. So he did do it, but I was very quick to make him withdraw, and I explained to him that was a really big sign of disrespect, and he could have back half of his donation. I politely told him that he could get dressed and when he was ready he could show himself out. I never saw him again after that, I refused his service. I went and got tested, and again about six months after that, and I was very, very lucky that everything came back negative. Like I said, I've never had a sexually transmitted disease, but it only takes a very small amount of time for that to change, so that was something that was a very, very surprising thing. This polite, gentle man was just so disrespectful. I mean it really forced me to stress it so that guys would be like, yes I get it, condoms are a must. I have this brand, this brand and this brand here. If none of those work for you, feel free to bring your own, but I will be inspecting them to make sure there was no tampering and they're not expired. The people who respect themselves, respect that. I had one gentlemen email me and say, "I hear that you're willing to do bareback," and I said, "Must have me mixed up with someone else, because I'm telling you now, there's absolutely no way that I'm ever providing full service to anyone. You could wave a thousand dollar bill in my face and you'll get the same answer. Condom or nothing."

Stress like this is not a regular part of the job for Hannah. Most of her experiences are fabulous, but emotions get tangly for her when she starts to think about the fact that many of her clients have spouses at home. She does not do sex work when she's in a relationship, yet somehow she manages to rationalize doing it with others who are married. "I'm reminded of that, and there's really someone getting hurt...I struggle with that. I feel a little hypocritical sometimes, particularly when the forty-something married male is the big contender amongst the population. There are the scattered gentlemen who are divorced. You sort of applaud them, you know, good for you, you don't want to get entangled in another sort of complicated situation right now."

In a small city like St. John's, there's a fairly high probability that one's status as a service provider or client will be discovered.[31] It's always in the back of Hannah's mind, especially since it happened to her once before and was very embarrassing for the individual who sought her out. So she tries to take more precautions. She does not engage in public sex or car dates. She maintains a low profile to outsiders and law enforcement, and she has never feared being charged or getting entangled in legal matters. She believes in the mentality shared amongst many service providers: cops have bigger fish to fry. If you're not causing anyone trouble, then who cares? The lines

---

31 During my research, I discovered that a few of my personal contacts have been engaging in this work at some time in their lives. These were revelations.

become greyed, however, when a service professional needs to seek law enforcement for her own protection. Hannah summarizes a story about a man, posing as a lesbian, who would frequent some of the massage parlours and abuse the women. He would stalk and threaten them. They knew his real name. Then the women would have to go to the police, tell them what they do for a living, and try to seek help from harassment.

"It reinforces the fact that I would never ever voluntarily tell anyone in my private life or personal life anything about it because you would get that same reaction. You don't know who you can trust. The only way to keep it a secret is to not tell anyone."[32]

32 At the time of publication, Hannah was taking a break from sex work.

"You have to be safe just like any other job. It's like someone collecting bloodwork. If you don't use gloves and use protection, you're going to get a disease, but if you're doing your job right, you'll be fine. You have to use safety precautions."

David is Candid

DAVID IS A MALE in his late forties who has been availing of sex services in St. John's for nearly three years. His services of choice are massage parlours and escorts, both local and foreign: "Pretty faces attached to petite bodies." He admits he's always been a bit awkward growing up and into adulthood, a self-proclaimed geek, so he never had much confidence or success in dating. He finds "paying for intimacy compensates somewhat for that history."

He finds escorts on the local adult-classifieds sites with the addition of word of mouth from some guys he's exchanged emails with about the women. He's replied to several online ads requesting information or discussing his experiences:

> First of all I evaluate the impartiality of the advertiser. A couple of times I've spoken to someone who clearly has some kind of vendetta against a particular woman. I am open about what I'm looking for. My own tastes run toward pretty, slim, and preferably petite, with BBBJ and CIM at the top of the list followed by DATY, DATO, and Greek.[33] My regular correspondents know this and look out for me. Also when I have an experience worth telling about, I will let them know, which sometimes prompts more recommendations back to me.

33 BBBJ refers to Bare Back Blow Job, CIM means Cum In Mouth, DATY is Dining at the Y (aka cunnilingus), DATO is Dining at the O (also known as analingus), Greek refers to anal sex.

He goes to the various places around town for other services: Ace Fantasies (now closed), Hush, Studio Aura, and Kendra's Red House.[34] The extra services some women at these establishments offer, in David's experience, are "CBJ[35], BBBJ (rarely and almost always unofficially), DATY, DATO, and finger penetration." David insists that it's not as seedy or underground as people may think.

> Parlour attendants especially are mainly just regular people trying to make a living. Sex work is a part of their lives, yes, but not necessarily a major part. That's also true of some SPs,[36] for whom the sex work is secondary to their otherwise perfectly normal lives. Before I knew better, I always thought of prostitution as a fulltime job, but that's not often the case for the women I like to see. Even the ones who travel here from away are not fulltime: I spoke to one girl from Quebec who comes here for the weekend every couple of months, just as a break from her day job.

Generally, there are three women in particular he sees on a regular basis outside of the massage parlours, all costing around $300/session.

There's a relationship blooming with one of them he met at a massage parlour—he admits he would have seen this woman three times a week if he could, but could only afford every week or two—even though there are strict rules about relationships. They're simply not allowed.

After helping this woman financially when times were difficult, they spent a lot of time together. It started with her hinting that she might be willing to meet outside her work for a casual sexual relationship. David jokes and chalks that up to his "outstanding DATY/DATO skills." With this particular woman, he realizes he is a stand-in for her long-absent father even though she would likely

---

34 Ace was rumoured to be a front for prostitution. Hush is considered very inexpensive: $110 for thirty minutes up to $150 for an hour. Rumour has it that some of the attendants at all of these places offer extras for $60-80 more, but it's definitely not part of the agreed upon public price.

35 CBJ: Covered Blow Job or oral sex with a condom.

36 Service Providers

never draw those conclusions herself. He realizes if they ever did have a *real* relationship, this might be a bit of a stumbling block.

The woman left her position at the massage parlour in 2015 and hasn't returned. While they still speak and are mutually attracted to each other, no real, public relationship has formed. He cannot book a hotel room or invite her over to his house because David is married with children. His wife has no idea of his extracurricular sexual activities, and he plans to keep it that way.

Obviously, he has no interest in getting caught by his wife or by law enforcement. While what he is doing—buying sex—is illegal in Canada, he does not fear getting caught, mostly because he chooses high-end escorts whom he knows with one hundred percent certainty are doing it of their own free will and are not being coerced or pimped.

David used to frequent Ace Fantasies until he surmised that the owner was pimping out the girls. In another situation, the one time David had an escort at his house, the sex worker got into an argument with her "driver" about how much money she was owed for her work. The man was clearly her pimp. If David suspects something of that nature, he does not engage with that individual anymore. Additionally, if an escort is obviously not enjoying herself, he won't call her again. He admits one girl seemed very eager at the beginning of their sexual relationship, and then as time passed, it was clear she was feeding an addiction: he had caught her injecting morphine, so he stayed away.

Given the personal and legal risks involved, the most obvious question anyone would ask is why? Why buy sex from someone when you're married and committed to another person? What's the payoff, and is it worth the stated risks? David is candid. He is dissatisfied at home and is no longer physically or sexually attracted to his wife. "My first experience was a matter of wanting to try something new, and experience a much younger woman. I always felt like I missed being with a girl my own age when I was in my late teens." The three women he sees make him feel "young and potent" and they seem to sincerely appreciate his company. "I understand it is a financial and sexual transaction, but the ones I go back to give me back something seemingly much deeper. I really feel appreciated for my sweet and sensitive personality and, yes, sexual skills." The risk for disease crosses David's mind regularly, but he uses protection for nearly everything with the exception of the occasional BBBJ with someone he trusts. He and his wife are no longer sexually active, so if he did get an infection or a disease, it would not be transmitted to her.

The legal ramifications are not worrisome. David admits he doesn't know much about Bill C-36. "I like to believe that I am somewhat protected by my care in choosing only escorts—I only see those that are really enthusiastic about what they do, and do not appear to have been coerced into the industry."

Truth be told, David fantasizes about life on his own and has contemplated leaving his wife on several occasions. He envisioned talking about it and later putting their house up for sale, getting an apartment with his girlfriend and so on, but he soon gave up on that idea.

> What's holding me back—besides lack of balls—is complicated, and there are a number of significant factors.[37] Financially it would be extremely hard on my wife, my kids would probably have difficulty forgiving me for doing it, my parents would not forgive me, similarly with my friends.

While there would be some financial advantages for David, he would miss the stability and certainty his current situation provides.

> There is quite a bit of convenience in keeping things as they are, even though sneaking around is obviously rather stressful. For example, tomorrow afternoon I

---

37 David shared a number of specifics with me during our correspondence, some of which will not be communicated in this piece because they would be clear identifier.

have an encounter planned with one of my favourite SPs, during which I will be taking clandestine time off work.

David regularly sees a psychiatrist who is not overly understanding of the situation. David describes him as "old school," saying he was "a bit shocked" and "disappointed." This is not anything David wants to hear as he's there for therapy and anti-depressant medication, not to be lectured.

> He has worked hard to convince me that there's no lack of love as such, so I conclude that I must be a jerk. I'm fundamentally a loner, even though I can be very loving at times. I honestly don't think I can be satisfied with one situation for more than a few years— at least, I haven't been. I'm not really sure how to explain it otherwise.

I FLAT OUT ASKED David if he feels that men who buy sex from women inherently disrespect them. "*Disrespect* is a bit of a vague word. I certainly objectify some women, and that is clearly disrespectful, but in my words and deeds I am kind and a perfect gentleman, and a great experience for the woman is always key to my own pleasure."

" I've been **smacked** many times.
Sure, I don't even **count** that. **"**

Everyone is Scamming

WHEN A MALE SEX worker asks you to come to his apartment for an interview, you say no. In fact, I said no anytime anyone asked me to come to their private dwelling for their interviews—male or female. Once I explained it was for safety reasons, they completely understood. Mostly. I only had one guy not return my emails. Fair enough. I did get two emails throughout the course of my research by "gentlemen" who wanted to "spend time with me." The man I was arranging to have coffee with for the purpose of an interview was not one of those creep shows. When I explained my intentions and why I wanted to meet in a public place, he just said, "That makes sense." Finally, I thought, this is a normal human being.

The Coffee Matters downtown is packed. Nearly every table is taken with the exception of two. A bald man sips his latte with his right hand while holding a thick trade paperback open with his left. I can't see the cover. His shirt has a brown stain on it the size of his thumb. I wonder if he knows. The barista with the dark glasses makes my vanilla latte and hands it to me without smiling, which seems an acceptable mode of customer service these days. It is okay not to smile. I assume he thinks smiling will somehow undermine his intellect.

So what do I know about this person I'm about to meet? I know he is an artist. He is friendly—at least his emails make me think so—and that is pretty much it. I have no idea who I am looking for when I sit down at the table kitty-corner to the main entrance at about five o'clock. It is the most private spot I can find. A large beam to my left shelters us from other patrons. I hope the chit chat and laughter combined with the aggressively calm jazz will mute our conversation within the space.

It is April. The first real nice day of the year. All the tables are taken and half of the patrons are triathlete types. A large man enters dressed in grey jogging pants and a white long-sleeve shirt, a small stain remembered on the sleeve. He stands there for a few seconds to catch his breath, wipes his brown hair from his pale, freckled face.

I wave, exhaling the nervous energy, and he sits down across from me at the two-person table. I didn't know that over the next hour and a half we would discover we had stuff in common, that he would make me laugh loudly with his wit, that he was the one who, six months prior, inspired the seeds of this project as the subject of a news piece about a sex worker who was gang raped in a downtown hotel.

MATT LOVES THE WORK he does. He says if you don't love it, you can't do it. While he loves it, it was not part of his life plan. He came upon this lifestyle randomly. One night a long time ago when he was in his early twenties, he got paid for sex. It surprised him. It surprised him, and it felt good. In recent years, disability has claimed him from traditional work, but he was working at the time of his first gig. That first gig turned into a regular thing. He makes outcalls and caters to men and women charging approximately $100 per session.[38]

It is probably one of the only industries where men automatically make less than women.

The money might be decent, but the cons are many. For Matt, "Stephen Harper and Peter McKay being assholes," is one of them, adding that sexual assault was also high on the list.[39] Rumour has it

---

38 The highest I've been told a person has been paid for one night is $1000.

39 Stephen Harper was the Prime Minister at the time and Peter McKay was the Minister of Justice and Attorney General. For more information on the legal perspective, see the educational pieces toward the end of the book.

that law enforcement, at the time of this interview, were not cracking down on prostitution in the city, but Matt refers to the new law. With that in mind, what the future holds is pretty unclear.[40]

While violence is not as big of a threat for Matt, because he's male and can be imposing when needed, he sympathizes with the women in the game. He feels that sex workers have no rights and that the current laws are sending people back to the streets, and "into alleys and it will likely go back to pimps and stuff, who are going to control girls with drugs."

Right now, girls can advertise on their own without the use of pimps. "They can be independent. A lot of people aren't forced into this life the way Conservative government would want a lot of people to believe."

Even so, he confirms there is human trafficking in this city, which is most obvious when there's a group of women in from Montreal or Toronto arriving and advertising at the same time. "The Russians," he says, "are usually trafficked." These girls are usually in a hotel room with one man, likely their pimp. "In this situation, I can guarantee you, someone's being trafficked. It is not a good scene. Many of the girls in the city, though, are doing it of their own free will."

Matt had a lot of opinions about politics, and he knew the laws inside and out. He spoke his opinions with confidence. It was when he spoke of an assault that his demeanor changed a little. He softened just a bit. His speech slowed and lowered. His eyes watered, but he didn't blink. I remembered the article about the hotel gang rapes in the fall of 2014. Matt was one of these victims.[41]

In the aftermath of that event, he takes extra precaution vetting clients and protecting himself. He's also still receiving treatments

---

40 Matt is referencing the passing down of Bill C-36. The controversy surrounding Bill C-36 is that it equates prostitution to human trafficking. It is hard to find any information on human trafficking in St. John's, but it exists. While not mutually exclusive with prostitution, it exists wherever prostitution exists.

41 While I haven't been able to confirm this, the rumour is that two other people were gang raped around this time at the same location.

and medical care to deal with the physical and emotional effects. When doing outcalls, he carries homemade mace, a special mixture of jalapeño juice and other household items. It will make you feel like you're in the ninth ring of hell, and it's not illegal.

His friends think he's overreacting and being overprotective, but having lived experience as a victim, he's always concerned about their wellbeing. "I keep trying to tell my friends to not accept drinks they didn't open, cause that's what happened to me. The next thing I know, I'm waking up outside a hotel."

People think male service professionals can defend themselves, which is false, particularly in the face of date-rape drugs or a weapon such as a handgun. Matt did have a gun pointed at him before, but he was quick to realize it was a fake. They had sprayed black paint over the orange tip. Matt laughs loudly when relaying this story to me, insulting the idiots who tried to scam him.

The women are not as lucky or as big as Matt. A couple of his female friends persist that it's safe sex or no sex, and then johns will take the condom off partially through the act, or say they're using one but won't. There are STDs that take months to show up, some even years.[42] Matt does not understand how anyone could take that risk. Diseases are not just passed between the service providers and their clients. Most of these guys have wives. Many people have drug habits. Many take unnecessary risks. Many people think acquiring an STD will never happen to them. Matt is hyper aware of the possible effects of any unprotected sex and thinks others should keep this top of mind too. "Everyone completely forgets about Tommy Sexton."[43]

Matt blames this lack of education on Conservative governments keeping religion in schools, something many believe should end. "I just don't like Stephen Harper. I think all the country agrees

---

42 The incubation period for most STDs is a few days to three months, but Molluscum Contagiosum and HIV can be dormant for up to six months (Boskey, "The Incubation Period of Common STDs").

43 Tommy Sexton was a comedian, born in St. John's, most recognized for his work on CODCO and as a member of The Wonderful Grand Band. He contracted AIDS and died from complications in 1993.

with me." Matt was right because, less than two years later, the Conservative government was voted out.

Matt wholeheartedly believes that legalization would benefit the economy and the workers similar to the outcomes from legalizing marijuana in some states.[44]

> The more you criminalize it, the more it's going to go underground. Consider Colorado, Washington, and California. They legalized marijuana and the rate of crime has dropped. I know attorneys, judges, and cops who smoke. People have to stop pretending they don't do other things. The public knows everyone's not innocent.

While Matt supports the rights of sex workers, he does not agree with the way sex workers were portrayed in the House during the consideration of Bill C-36, specifically referencing the Dominatrix, Terri Jean Bedford, who appeared before the House donning leather and dragging a whip. While he agreed with her plight, not so much the dramatic and explicit way it was expressed, he feels as though this exaggerated portrayal makes everyone look bad and becomes more of an embarrassment, something that, in the long run, doesn't do anyone any good. "People forget that we are real people."

Real people don't need to make statements, they need to make money. Seldom can someone survive on disability payments alone. There's no wonder people find unconventional ways to make money. Matt firmly states that if not for sex work, he would be homeless.

While the Safe Harbour Outreach Project (SHOP) provides many needed services to sex workers in the city—such as a the Warn Other Workers (WOW) hotline, condoms, emotional support, and more—it is not enough in a booming city like St. John's, where more and more people are offering and availing of these types of

---

44 At the time this piece was written, recreational and medicinal marijuana was legal in Alaska, Colorado, Oregon, and Washington. Medical and recreational marijuana was legal in the following cities: Portland, South Portland, and Keego Harbor. Decriminalization laws existed in twelve states. Canada is now set to legalize marijuana by July of 2018.

services.[45] While there are a multitude of resources available to drug addicts, Matt would like to see the same consideration given to sex workers.

Stigma plays a large part in that discrepancy. No one wants to come out to random people about their relationship to sex work. People are rarely understanding and accepting. The relationship between sex worker and client is also a strange one. Matt describes it as "a very unique perspective on human nature. Some people are very weird. Some are very nice. Some just want to talk. Some think that just because you're in this job, you're too stupid to have another job, and they can pull the wool over your eyes so fast." He goes on to recount a story of a friend who was nearly scammed because someone said they left their wallet in the back of their jeep. He fears that if he wasn't there, his friend would have been victimized.

It's no surprise that scams come with the territory—scams, punching, weird requests. Matt keeps telling his friends they need to get the money upfront, all of it. There are times when people do not want to pay upfront and problems can arise. "I try not to cause problems. I try to resolve it nicely. Once I wanted to punch somebody, but that's about it. He was a former cop, so I put my hand back in my pocket."

Another prevalent scam is the picture collector, which is something I did not consider before starting this project. Basically, someone posing as a potential client will engage a sex worker online and ask for their picture and then discontinue the communication. "You can spot them a mile away," says Matt. "You send them a face shot and then a body shot and they want more pictures. No, that's not happening. It's a waste of time." The picture collector then uses the images for arousal without the service professional getting paid.

Matt has friends who wait for calls and then spend half an hour on the phone with the john. For Matt, this is a waste of time because

---

45 SHOP provides support for women and men who engage in sex work or survival sex in St. John's and surrounding areas. They offer non-judgmental supportive services, safety or exit planning, referrals, harm reduction items, and more. At the time of publication, a new program was just starting to help sex workers exit.

it's obvious what's going on there. They're getting what they want without having to pay. Not everyone is as seasoned as Matt. He feels bad seeing his friends being taken advantage of in so many ways.

> Everyone is scamming, and then some of the girls are really catty. They'll get their friends or boyfriends to put up a fake warning on the websites about other girls.[46] There's money to be made. Some do better than others. The ones that aren't doing well are the ones that are doing drugs because they do a call and it's going up their arm.

Matt is clean and has never dabbled in street drugs. Alcohol was once a problem for him, but no longer.

> Alcohol is the most legal drug, and drunk drivers are more dangerous than stoners. I was at least a smart alcoholic. I never got behind the wheel. I'll have a social drink now and then, and by now and then I mean once a year, and it's two drinks tops. So I went completely cold turkey. I don't believe God can save you from addiction, that's AA bullshit. I have to be sober. That's the only way I can be normal.

He has a close friend who is addicted, and he fears he will soon get a call saying she's dead. It takes her two hours to find a vein, and she can't do a call without it. Having tried to help in numerous ways, he has exhausted his options. He believes people shouldn't do this work if they have drug addictions because the more money they get, the more drugs they do. "I'm surprised more sex workers haven't shown up dead."

Yes, there are drug addicts among the sex-worker population, but not everyone is a drug addict. Not everyone is a home wrecker. Not everyone was abused when they were a child. Not everyone has an STD. "We are normal. We're not criminals like some people may

---

46 Matt is referencing the adult-service sites such as *Backpages, Craigslist* and *NL Adult.*

think. It's just a job. When I was traditionally working, I was good at what I did. I got paid. It's the exact same thing." Many people do not share Matt's liberal opinion.

Having many political views, Matt takes this opportunity to vent. "We need more good services. We need people to not judge us so harshly. Like the feminists."

Feminism's relationship with sex work is complex. Each feminist can have different views on the origins of sex work, the effects, and so on. Some feminists think sex work is a symptom of the inequality inherent in the patriarchal order. Some feminists believe women should have the right to choose what they do with their bodies regardless of what that is. And still other feminists engage in sex work themselves and find it empowering. Matt believes this is feminism at work. "It's not men taking advantage of women. It's if you want this, you're going to pay a large amount of money."

He also takes issue with Child Youth and Family Services for the way they treat sex workers. "It's not the best profession, but it's not like they're bringing clients home with the kids in the apartment. The kids are with the babysitter, and the moms are gone to the studio or wherever. It's a job." He used to babysit for one of his friends. He would stay there in the night, get the kid up and ready for school, feed them, and get them out the door. Matt believes that education would lead to realizations:

> They'd realize the girls are empowered, they're making money, they're in control. It's not like the guys are coming in and saying we're going to do this, this, and this. The girls are the ones that say it's $500.

He references the popularity of BDSM work across the country.[47] "So you're going to pay me $500 and I'm going to treat you like the dog you are? Ok. I can do that." He laughs about the odd stuff he's had to put up with. "It sounds weird but the only thing I've

---

47 BDSM stands for Bondage, Discipline, Sadism and Masochism which includes Dominance and Submission practices. "Hidden Behind the Orgasm" dives into this side of sex work.

really been proud of while doing this is that I got assaulted." He immediately took action and warned other workers, which likely saved some from being raped.

> Enough's enough. We have to warn people. It happened at a hotel. What you heard in the news, I was one of them. I was the only male. I was okay with the media knowing on one count only, that they used "sex worker" not "prostitute" or "hooker" or any of that. It's "sex worker," "service provider." Mine would be "sex expert." They didn't listen though. They used "prostitute."

SHOP was a huge support for Matt during this time, and did what they could to help him. They tried to get him to speak to law enforcement, but he opted not to do that. "At least I was strong enough not to go back to booze." He walked to the liquor store the day after and stood there in the whisky aisle staring at a twenty-six-ounce bottle of Jack Daniels.

> I was later told that I likely saved at least three other girls by sharing my story with the help line. I'd lay down my life to save someone. I gave up my health to save three women. I got something to be proud of doing this. I'm glad I can't remember anything about it. I was roofied. I can vaguely remember seeing a room number. I can remember waking up. I was walking. On my way home. As a guy, I didn't want to go to a doctor. I knew I had to. I had to. But I think I'm damaged. The blood work has come back clean so far. I'm almost near the six-month mark.[48]

---

[48] After the six month mark, Matt was happy and relieved to receive a clean bill of health.

"I worked at a massage parlour, and obviously, I have no problem with the idea of them or **strip clubs,** but I believe they shouldn't be allowed in **residential** areas.**"**

This is Not an Offer of Prostitution

JESSICA AND DANIEL ARE a married couple in their thirties living in an affluent suburb of St. John's. The last time they were without gym memberships was in their early twenties while in university. Their day jobs clear well over six figures. They are the picture of "normal" life, except they secretly offer sensual massage out of their modern west-end home.

After toying with the swinging lifestyle[49] and finding pleasure there, someone nonchalantly said their massage skills coupled with their good looks and firm bodies could make them some money. They thought about it. Who couldn't use a little extra money?

While they were at it, they serviced clients one to four times a month, mostly married, middle-aged men and younger men, all exploring their bisexual side. Initially they had hoped for women and couples, but the interest just wasn't there. They could have serviced more but were quite particular about those they entertained—they wanted physically fit individuals willing to pay a hefty price. If they weren't picky, they admit, they could have made much more money.

They offered services out of their home for two years before taking a break. Respected in their jobs and feeling, like many in this industry, that they have a lot to lose, it became a little too risky. "It's very nerve

---

49 Rumours of swingers clubs in and around St. John's is nothing new. Some are said to have 300+ members.

wracking having someone come to your house and not know if you might know each other, whether they might be friends, family, co-workers, or the police." Not knowing the background of these strangers was also stressful. No one in Jessica and Daniel's lives know they engage in this activity either professionally or personally. "Not a flipping chance," said Jessica. "My God, I'd die."

While they, unlike almost all others I've interviewed, have never been in harm's way, they have had some awkward experiences with clients. One person backed out when they were undressed and the massage had commenced. "It was the weirdest experience ever," said Jessica. "I kinda said, 'Are you okay? Did we do something wrong?' He apologized profusely and left." He had already paid them in advance, so she offered him half of his money back, but he said no.

> I guess he got spooked. Ironically, he emailed us back a month later and asked if we'd perform S&M on him. He wanted kink. We were floored and said no. If he backed out when we massaged him, we weren't going to do anything else with him. Had he said he wanted to try the massage again, I would have gave him another chance.

The agreement they send to their prospective clients is thorough and portions of it read like legalese. It ensures everyone knows what to expect, and more importantly, what not to expect. Jessica reiterates that they must agree to the terms before any appointment is made, terms that state the $300/hr charge is for massage only. It is not an offer of prostitution. No fees or tips of any kind are quoted in exchange for any illegal sexual conduct. Further contact with them constitutes acceptance of those terms. The understanding being that if they engage in sexual activity after the session, it is a personal matter between consenting adults and is not a part of any contract.

They direct prospective clients to their favourite porn sites, express their interest in exhibitionism as well as voyeurism and require them to send a photo pre-booking to establish attraction and protect their own anonymity.

While their friends and family have no idea about their swinging lifestyle or this unorthodox service offered out of their suburban neighbourhood home, they love exploring these sensual sides of themselves and others. While it's not for everyone or every couple, it worked for them and their relationship. They are unsure if it will be part of their future.

"A lot of the girls will steal **wedding rings**. The guys will take them off and put them in the console. Then the girl will **paw** it. The wife will pretty much report it stolen, find it at the pawn. shop and **know** where it came from."

Hitting the Jackpot

IT WAS A PERFECT winter day in February. Cold, sunny, wide-open sky. The Tim's on Torbay Road was packed with families returning from sliding at Pippy Park. The tile floor offered puddles of melted snow that people walked in to get around the "Caution: Wet Floor" pylons. The line was out the door. Upon arrival, I knew which stranger I was looking for. She was the lone woman seated amongst tables of groups. Her dirty blond hair hung to the middle of her back, her lipstick was the colour of a new bruise. She sat with her back straight and had a small spiral notebook in front of her on the table. It was filled with cursive notes in blue ink. She leaned in and shook my hand as I sat down. We began by talking about her childhood, one that needed no telling as it was "very regular." No abuse. No neglect. No dirty secrets.

Vanessa is a transgender woman who does sex work from her home. At the time of the interview, she was new to sex work. The first two months were strictly exploratory, but when she made enough money to survive for two more months without having to work a regular job, she committed.

Having just started her transition from male to female in her early thirties, which is considered a little late, she needed a job that could help her pay for expensive medical treatments and surgeries. After six months of "solid consideration," she decided to try sex work. "When I first put up my name, my ad, my email would explode. I probably got individual people, well over one hundred, contacting me."

"I deal with a fairly specific group of people," said Vanessa. "I'm not a call girl. I mostly do in-calls. They come to me." At the time of the interview, Vanessa did not do outcalls but was considering it. There's a higher risk when leaving the comfort and safety of your home. "After I heard about that [hotel gang rape], in-calls seem to be the best. See, I know who's coming to my house. I know who's in my house. If I look out my door and see five people, I cannot even open it or I can let one in and lock it behind him. And I know my way around my house." Vanessa has never been victimized or threatened. Doing the work at home might have something to do with that. It also allows her to increase the donation amount, which means her clients are more upscale. They possibly have more to lose if they are ever caught. It also might have something to do with how she vets her johns. It starts with them answering an ad followed by an email exchange, which many sex workers feel can reveal a lot about a person. The johns know they are soliciting a transgender woman when they initiate contact. Because this is a niche market, most of those who come to Vanessa are seeking a first-time experience, something experimental, or the answer to a lifelong fantasy.

> I don't get people who work minimum-wage jobs. I get people with high-paying jobs. They'll come and pay for an hour. I don't do half hours. Like people have asked, sent me an email just looking for a blow job, and I'm like, "No, I don't do that" because it's just not worth my time. For a lot of people, I'm fulfilling an insane fantasy. Many guys are so cute. They're really shy, and a few of them are quite attractive. You wouldn't think they'd be shy or nervous, but they are. I have to talk them down.

These experiences, coupled with the money, have made Vanessa fall in love with the work. "I love it. I really do. I love my job. I even call it my job. I quit my real job to do this."

Some sessions border on dates. They hook up the PlayStation, cook meals, talk. Relationships develop. She has five regulars now. One guy returns every few months and pays for three hours at a time. They eat and catch up. It's not just sex. "He's one of these guys who doesn't get a lot of time. He's so busy. I guess finding a woman is pretty difficult, and he likes transgender women. It's not just a fetish for him. It's his woman. And he wants to come back. It's good to not have to rush."

Most of her clients are "quite wealthy," many have wives and children, and they range in age from twenty-eight to sixty. She has yet to turn anyone down, but would if she didn't want to go through with the session. Her one big requirement is that people are clean. Not too much to ask. "If you come in and you smell, you're either going home or you're going in my shower." One guy showed up and asked if he could shower first. "Yes, please. Twice. Here's eight bars of soap."

No one in Vanessa's private life has ever contacted her, even unwittingly, to request her services, but she, unlike other women, is open to that.

> I think it would be awesome. I had a guy once who thought he did know me, but I told him, "Not a chance." I don't have a lot of friends. And even if he did, what does it matter? If someone I knew showed up, they'd get the red-light special. I'd be that much more relaxed. It hasn't happened yet. It's funny because I get a lot of stories about disappointments. For a good while I wasn't putting my face up [posting her image on the web]…I didn't at first, anyway, and people would get concerned that they would show up and see a guy with lingerie on. I have had several guys say that that exact thing had happened to them. Sometimes guys ask me if I go out like this, and I tell them, "This is me." If you see me in the Avalon Mall, here I am. They're used to getting crossdressers but not a transgendered woman. Because of that I'm picking up so many regulars because they come to my house and they're like, this is exactly what I'm looking for for my fantasy.

The money and free time are some of the benefits for Vanessa, but the biggest pro is the way it makes her feel. As a transitioning woman, she can't think of anything else that could be more gender confirming. It makes her feel as though she's made the right decision—a sentiment many transgender sex workers feel. It's "empowering, satisfying," and has improved her emotional well-being according to her therapist. Being allowed to be feminine, to be wanted as a woman, was like hitting the identity jackpot.

The purpose behind the choice was to make money for expensive surgeries and treatments, procedures that are not necessarily covered by MCP or insurance. Generally some of the surgeries trans women want are electrolysis, top surgery, bottom surgery, and tracheal shave. While Vanessa doesn't necessarily know that she wants all of these procedures, the ones she wants cost thousands of dollars. The main surgery she is saving for is top surgery.[50] Bottom surgery is in a whole other ballpark because of the hoops one has to jump through such as years of therapy and the raising of thousands of dollars. She is considering a tracheal shave to heighten her voice, but opted to see a speech therapist in the short term to help her sound more feminine.[51]

She has made a long mental checklist of the surgeries and treatments she needs to reach her end goal of being the fully formed transgender woman she feels is right for her. Therapy is now checked off that list. Her therapist concluded the journey two years ago because Vanessa no longer needed it.

Her therapist provided a good sounding board for processing some feelings on the challenges of transitioning and her entrance into sex work, which was a necessary partnership. While Vanessa is becoming more and more open about her sex work, not many of her family members or friends know. She has told a select few for safety and security reasons only.

---

50 At the time of publication, Vanessa reported her top surgery had been completed.

51 A feminine speech pattern or voice usually has more versatility than a male pattern. Topics are more personal, women tend to use more persuasive language than men, and they play with sounds more than men (Bennett, *Feminist Fight Club*).

Current law states that it's illegal for anyone to live off the avails of prostitution, which means sex workers cannot hire security guards, at least not legally. The one bonus of working from an agency or house with others is this added protection. Until prostitution is fully legal, it's hard to navigate the waters of what is criminal and what is decriminalized, what is legal and what is not.[52]

If it was legal, Vanessa's life would become a hassle. "All of a sudden I'm running my own business, and that involves taxes and all sorts of things. It would be a pain in the ass for me, but I'd still like it to be legalized." If it was legalized, there would be an avenue for legal recourse if she was ever victimized.[53] "Where it's illegal right now, everything is under the table, we can't do anything about it." This summarizes the conundrum many sex workers feel about legalization.[54]

The Safe Harbour Outreach Project is the first program in St. John's that offers support to sex workers. Vanessa avails of these services and is thankful that she and other workers have someone in their corner. Before SHOP was up and running in 2011, they had no help.

Vanessa's private challenges have motivated her to become active in St. John's, advocating for women's, sex worker, and trans rights. She never misses the annual Slut Walk, walks in Take Back the Night, and voices her opinions in panel discussions on sex-worker rights. Being a well-spoken, educated trans woman with a unique perspective, she feels compelled and will continue to use her voice in whatever way she can to advocate for the rights of her demographic.

---

52 For answers to legal questions regarding sex work, please see the Q&A toward the back of the book.

53 There were only a few commonalities amongst the stories, this statement being one of them.

54 Cheryl Auger accurately summarizes this, in "Bill C-36: No Safety or Security for Sex Workers," when she writes, "The Bill claims to view sex workers as victims, yet it also considers sex workers as threatening to communities. It's very difficult to think of another group that is considered both victims in need of state protection and as threats to the community to be contained by the state."

"I can't really describe it. It's everything. You're confident, you feel like you're gorgeous and sexy, and you're being paid for it and you're making more money than you ever could and you're having so much fun with it. It's like being famous and rich and everything. I'm addicted to it."

Hidden Behind the Orgasm

IN ORDER TO FIND someone in the fetish world that would talk to me for the book, I had to join an online fetish community and reach out to some big players across the island. I got some advice from a man in Corner Brook who has embraced the BDSM lifestyle, who told me to join some groups within that community.[55] After posting a write-up about the research, I got a few responses. Grace called me on a Saturday afternoon.

"It's a very interesting separation to live in two worlds," she said during our introductory conversation. Over the next hour she educated me on the lifestyle, the lingo, and her experience as a professional dominant or ProDom. There is a large Community in this province, as well as worldwide, of people who appreciate BDSM and kink. In the simplest terms possible, it's largely for people who enjoy taking control or relinquishing control in various ways which includes spanking, bondage, gagging, flogging, etc. It can be relationship-based or just for fun.[56]

Grace's choice to be a ProDom—to receive payment for her BDSM services—adds a layer of complexity.

> I don't get involved with the community part of it. While kink and BDSM are a big part of my sexuality,

---

55 Apparently the west coast (Corner Brook and Deer Lake particularly) has a relatively large BDSM community compared to the size of the local population.

56 I asked a few people who are into BDSM what they thought of *Fifty Shades of Grey*, and they all came back with the same opinion: that it's nowhere near the reality of what it means to embrace a Dominant/Submissive lifestyle and is an amateur introduction at best.

> power-exchange relationships have become a job for me, not play. When you add money to the mix, you're doing it for pay, and then you're doing it at the whim and desire of whomever is there in front of you. They want what they pay for.[57]

Her experience with kink is that there are people who dabble, there are people who play and get involved with groups to have a little kinky fun, and there are people who embrace it as a lifestyle—they are dominants or submissives (or sometimes both) who remain in those roles outside the bedroom. Grace is a consultant for those who want to learn more and embrace the lifestyle.

> I have people who are regular clients on a monthly basis who I have worked with on an ongoing level to be their Dom. They would be afforded certain allocations of my time: certain amounts of contact, there were certain things they had to do. All very individualized plans and specific to their needs, wants, desires, and circumstances. So it wasn't the casual one-time encounter that most pros handle. Some of them went on for years; long-term relationships that you just happened to get paid for.

Grace started this work in 2003 and has had several long-term clients. She admits she's grown up with some of the men. There have been major life experiences happening in the background on both sides, such as marriages, births of children, divorces, and so on. She did engage in the individual session now and then to make some extra money. These one-time sessions would often be fetish work such as humiliation, caning, or bondage. She would provide services for an hour or two and get paid $300-$500 at the end. To arrange meetings, she would engage the individual via email and hope her gut instinct was right. Sometimes things would go wrong and she would have to fall back on contingency plans. "There's some people that I've cancelled because I just got a really kind of weird vibe, and there are people that I should have cancelled but didn't."

---

57 There's an opinion held by some in the BDSM community which suggests that unless there's some sort of intercourse or some sort of actual sex, it isn't really sex work. If you're flogging someone or making them crawl around, is that sex?

Generally, the one-time appointments are playground-level fetish work for Grace, work she does for "amusement" and a little extra cash. She has attended fetish nights at local bars and can easily pinpoint the fakers, people carrying floggers when they would have no clue how to swing them. She enjoys the theatre of it though, and understands that people like to think they're naughty.[58]

The long-term engagement with someone is a whole other thing. She learns the personal details of their lives and tries to decipher what they need opposed to what they think they want. "True D/S," says Grace, "is more about the mind fuck than the body fuck." You need to have a thorough, accurate understanding of the individual's life, their everyday life, their challenges, and so on. Thus, confirming contracts with longer-term clients can be arduous.

> It's more of a negotiation. Initial contact would be made through email or one of the online groups or things like that. I had a couple discrete ads in a few little places. Some people would email me and we would chat, we would talk about really normal things as if it was a first date. It wouldn't really venture out into anything too sexual or too kinky because I wanted to know who they were, the type of person they were, and I can be picky. If I didn't like them as a person, I didn't take them on as a client.

Even with a rigorous screening process, it wasn't always easy to tell if someone might be potentially violent.

> Anyone who has been assaulted or raped, no matter what the circumstances, it's awful, but, and this is going to sound really bad, but on some level you get used to it, because it happens with disturbing regularity. Not necessarily the explosive, gang-raped-in-a-hotel-room kind of situation, but the smaller things. I'll give you a couple of examples. When I was taking on clients, I

---

58 I heard that during one of these nights a few years back, a person showed up who claimed to be in the lifestyle. They sat there, giggled, and smirked through the party, and then wrote an article about it without having talked to anyone.

would email first and then speak on the phone. If that went well, we would meet for coffee. So there were a few opportunities to get to know somebody before I was ever in a private room with them. There was a man once where we had progressed through all of those steps and I had met him at his home here in the city while the wife and kids were away. We were sitting down and I had asked him to strip and kneel for me because that is often the first request I make. After he did so, he grabbed me and pushed me down and orally raped me. Then, here I am in this stranger's home. It's his home. You recognize the position you're in. You recognize that you are a sex worker, you are a kink worker; that there is no purpose and point in going out and screaming rape. There is nobody coming to help, so you plan to get out of it and escape as quickly as you can. The easiest way to get out alive is to detach from it and not be hysterical. It sounds really cold doesn't it?

I told Grace that, in fact, in that situation, it sounded like survival instinct. She continued:

I've been raped two or three times. I've been assaulted, depends on what you classify as assault—when you're in that intimate environment and someone reaches up and grabs at you, do you consider that an assault? I don't know. As a Dom you are paid to hurt people, sometimes they hurt back. Sometimes it's an instinct and sometimes it's malicious, but you're paid to hurt people and, you know, sometimes things cross the line.

There are many lines that are crossed in this work, some physical and others emotional. Grace has these intimate experiences, sometimes borderline violent, sometimes unwanted interactions with men who have wives and children, and then she sees them on the news or around the city.

Trying to decipher who people are, what they're capable of, takes skill. Sizing people up quickly, knowing the signs, observing body language and eye contact, are some of the tactics Grace uses, all the while being hesitant and cautious.

> People never get to know who I am. I am the listener. I am the secret keeper. Even in my own personal relationships. Even in friendships. Even in vanilla ordinary situations. I've become the person that people share with but that I don't share with other people, and it gives me an interesting sort of power because I know everybody's dirty little business. There are people in this city who we see on the television on a fairy regular basis, there are people who are provincial leaders and community leaders that just happened to like getting strapped down and getting things shoved up their ass. There are men that like being diapered and behaving like little babies. There are men that love being forced to dress up in slutty women's underwear and being taken out for a drive, all because their entire daily existence revolves around them being in control themselves and they're so fucking desperate to give it up. And the more power and control someone has, the more intense the depths of their need to submit has been. I'll give you an example: I remember sitting in a McDonald's and I met with a gentlemen who walked in larger than life in his $3000 suit, Rolex watch, and when he walked in, the whole place stopped and turned their head because he had that sort of presence, and I was sitting there in the grubbiest of clothes, and I don't generally do grubby, but it was to prove a point. I'm sitting there in a hoodie and jeans and he comes over and he grovels. He asks if he's allowed to sit, so I let him stand for a while next to the table. Here's this man who could buy and sell me 50, 100, 1000 times over and he's begging for permission to be able to sit next to me. There's nobody in this entire restaurant that can

understand the dynamic of what's going on here, they just think it's some guy standing next to some girl who's far below his class and his category, but what they don't know is, I own him. He's mine. If I ask him to kneel right here in this spot right now even in all his riches and power, he will kneel right in the middle of McDonald's for me because he's mine.

Grace chalks this up to psychology, not sex. It's about the dynamics of power and the ability to trust.

Every person craves acceptance for who and what they are, and it is more fundamental than just sex and orgasm. It is an intimacy and a closeness and they want a buddy to tell them that they're okay, that they're loveable, and they are wonderful people even if they do like being pissed on. While the sex and the various fetishes and all of those things are fun and the sex is fun, you try to push yourself as far as you can to do something different. If somebody is face down on my floor with their ass up in the air with their ass cheeks spread and I am five fingers deep and halfway to my wrist inside their ass, they better be able to trust me because if not, somebody's getting hurt. It is about pushing yourself to trust someone so implicitly.

Grace believes that trust is a big part of every aspect of sex work, and that many sex workers feel like therapists who deal with the problems everyday people have regarding intimacy, closeness, and acceptance, all of which is largely hidden behind the orgasm.

Every single person she meets wants somebody to tell them they're okay, tell them they're not freaks, that even though they enjoy strange things, things that would make some shudder, it's okay:

For example, there are men that like being my own personal toilet. There are men that like being choked. There are men that like a good thrashing or whatnot and like to have their penises caned.[59] There are times where, as a Dom, you are pushed beyond your own limits as well. I like hurting people, but I don't want to harm people. That's a fine distinction, but it is an enormous one.

Some will come to you and they'll want to be punished, desperately want to be punished for their life successes, and they have this weird sense of guilt where they have all the success and all the money that they achieved. They want to be treated like shit, and they want to be humiliated, and they want to be beaten, or they want to be cuckolded or all sorts of very different things, and they want to be embarrassed or humiliated because there's some sort of penance involved, but ultimately they still want to think that they're okay. I find them all very endearing, every single man that I've ever taken on, especially the long-term ones, they all matter to me. And their wellbeing matters to me. If not, I would never have gotten into any sort of long-term relationship-for-pay thing.

Being a therapist of sorts for others, Grace has to invest in her own self-care and emotional wellbeing. To ensure she remains intact, she writes, works out, whips people, which sounds strange but is cathartic for her:

The whipping and the paddling and the caning, they're very athletic activities. They take energy. They build sweat and all sorts of those physical outcomes. You also need some person that you can vent to. The expectations that come with being paid, the commitments involved, especially when you deal with high-stakes money, are high. The consulting clients I had were paying a lot of money. We're not talking a $20 blow job, we're talking sometimes $2000 a month. That wasn't on a per-session basis. We are negotiating a

59 Refers to being hit with a bamboo cane. The harder the hit, the harder the erection.

contract and you will pay me this amount monthly. It isn't always $2000, depending on how much people wanted, but if they wanted some significant chunk of my time, they are certainly paying for it because I offer something that is pretty exclusive and unique. The men expect a certain level of professionalism and a certain level of, this sounds awful because it shouldn't be true, but they expect a certain perceived level of class and decorum and intelligence and background and breeding, and all the foolishness that can come with expectations like that. They want to be able to think that you are smarter than they are and that you are more capable than they are; that you are more in control than they are because, again, it's that illusion— if it breaks, it all falls apart. And it takes a certain level of theatre to be able to pull that off. You need to be aware of your surroundings because they will ask you what is going on with x, y, z oil merger or the crisis in such-and-such country and you have to be able to match them at their own game and beat them at their own game. It is a high-stakes game with high-stakes players because, you know, your regular Bob from Mount Pearl is certainly not going to be able to explain away a couple thousand dollars a month to the wife.

When Grace first started out, she had an advisor, someone who works in the business, and they told her she needed to value her time, advising that if she lowered her price, she wouldn't get high-end clientele. This was the best guidance she received because it automatically deemed her services luxurious, special, and elite. Much of mainstream culture has taught us that these services are not special, but are deviant, and those who engage are ultimately scary and weird. In Grace's lived experience, over more than a decade, this is 100 percent not the case:

People think those of us involved in the BDSM lifestyle are all dirty deviants: leather clad, hiding in bars and basements. They would probably be alarmed to know just how common it is. There is, for such a small province, an enormous BDSM community. It is huge and it is far-reaching. There are some towns in Newfoundland and Labrador that have a lot of kink happening; pockets of activity all over.

One of the advantages of this lifestyle is that it has given Grace immense practical knowledge of human beings and psychology. It's helped her understand and appreciate her individual power, and enabled her to unleash her creativity and exert her control in ways she never imagined. She was also able to explore the darkest corners of her desires without involving her spouse or bringing it anywhere near her children. Going outside of her marriage for these experiences has enabled her to satisfy desires without making her home life uncomfortable. The money is the other obvious advantage. The ego trip, as Grace puts it, is another benefit. "It's really something to mess with people's heads and bodies. I walk around like the queen of the world sometimes. I do. It's true."

The downside is that it's difficult to completely understand yourself, and the compartmentalizing can be exhausting. Thoughts and emotions become hard to untangle. Grace can be uber-professional in her day job, be the high-class ProDom in her afterhours life, or the loving spouse and mother. Trying to mesh those can become complicated. Uncertainty about who your true self is becomes a normal feeling. Another drawback is the safety risk, but ultimately, what Grace really fears is being outed. It would destroy her life, her career, her family; her clients' lives would be destroyed. There is a lot to lose for everyone involved. For this very reason, she does not do one-off outcalls anymore.

The risk of being outed is so real for Grace that she said she would immediately regret doing this interview. "I have walked into countless hotel rooms not knowing what was on the other side of the door, but making this phone call today was just as scary."

" I've been to jail before, but never for prostitution. **"**

Sloshed

I GOT TOGETHER WITH a few women who have worked or are currently working in strip clubs as bartenders. I won't reveal their names. They had a lot of little tales to tell about what they've seen and surmised about the strip-club world as women who have birds-eye views on a somewhat secretive industry.

One girl started bartending in the sports-bar area of the Cotton Club and eventually moved upstairs where the tips were better and the men were nastier.

> I could serve someone all night in the sports bar and then see them upstairs and they would be a completely different person. They would think they could get away with saying certain things to me. They would never say that to me on the sports bar in the same outfit, but they're upstairs surrounded by the nudity.

The inhibitions are down and the objectification is up.

Apparently, the older men are the worst ones. Most of the young guys go to George Street to get what they're looking for. It's the older, married ones who go for a night out to look at young, naked women.

One bartender has overheard customers confessing that they just "finger banged" a girl or that someone "just got a blow job" upstairs, which is not allowed. "You don't need a condom for a lap dance.

Your clothes are on." From talking to the manager, this is not a part of the sex industry the Cotton Club wants any part of. Any strip club that endorses this behaviour is participating in illegal activity. But what goes on under the cover of darkness when drinking is involved is anybody's guess. Boundaries can be pushed and sometimes even bulldozed.

"I mean if a guy comes down and he had a blowjob upstairs, he is definitely going home and telling twenty of his friends that it happened, and then people are coming in and almost expecting it." This is unfair to the dancers who are not providing that service:

> You have these gorgeous girls who are beautiful, but you see this particular girl who's always going upstairs [to the lap-dance area] and she's alright. Why is everyone taking her? And then you put two and two together. She's doing extras. It's shitty because it frustrates the strippers.

While there are wooden panels separating the booths in the private lap-dance area of the bar, if you stand up you can see what's going on beside you. This creates a lot of friction between the girls.

"Then guys that are here fairly often are asking for particular girls, and it's like, why the hell are you taking her? She's half chubby, wears her hair in a ponytail, no makeup." It comes down to money. The dancers are there to make money and they will sometimes get that money by unsavoury means.

"A lot of them are thieving," said one bartender. If a dancer is giving a guy a private lap dance, he may stay upstairs longer than expected and will need to go to the ATM to pay her. The dancer follows him to the ATM to ensure he doesn't run off, hovers around while he's getting his cash out, picks up on the pin number, steals his wallet, and could ultimately clean him out. Not every dancer is like this, of course, but the girls agree they've seen it many times before.

As far as the customers go, they run the whole gamut. Men ranging from nineteen to eighty, men with disabilities both physical and mental, men from all over the world and every pocket of the island.

The sad reality about the majority of the strippers, said one bartender, is that many are sex workers. It seems not many have pimps. Some are doing it because they know they can make money. If paying attention, it's easy to tell who has a pimp and who doesn't. Their spending habits are a telltale sign. Girls who are forth-coming with their money and are drinking, buying shots, they don't have pimps. The ones showing up really early are potentially "owned" because they have to be there a lot in case he's checking in. Rumour has it that the girls who come from away, who travel together three to four at a time, are the ones who have pimps. One girl is usually more dominant than the others, has more say in what they're doing at the bar, particularly when it comes to drinking. Because so many of them drink, a woman who is making her own money doesn't look to someone else and ask if they can buy another drink. She goes to the bank machine. She gets drunk if she wants to.

Most of the girls have to be sloshed to get on stage. They drink before they come to work, drink during, take shots, and get completely annihilated. Of course, how do you do it otherwise? How do you get on stage, get naked, dance, and be completely sober?

Drug addictions are also prevalent.[60] Certain girls will flock to certain guys—dealers—when they come into the bar. "If you're generally sober and tending bar, you can see these things happening around you, and you can see people get higher and higher as the night progresses." There's usually only one or two dancers who really get out of hand. One bartender remembers a girl who was so out of her mind about five years ago, she fell down the stairs, ripped her two knees open, went into the bathroom, and proceeded to fix her make-up, completely unaware that blood was dripping down

---

60 The most popular drugs right now are morphine, Dilaudid, cocaine, Ritalin, Percocet, and opiates in general.

both legs. She needed stitches. Sadly, that night, she left with five men. They were talking about "taking her with them." Years later she was found dead.

Nowadays it's hard to tell if people are truly out of it, mostly due to the prevalence of prescription drugs. With cocaine, there are certain giveaways like grinding your teeth or excessive sniffing. Some girls do MDMA[61] recreationally, but all bartenders agree it's not a huge problem as of yet.

While these bartenders find the job a little stressful dealing with drunks, objectification, and the occasional fight, they admit the tips are worth it, and can make up to $1000 a night when times are good.

61 Also known as Molly or ecstasy.

"I genuinely **care** for many of my **clients**."

We Are Recession Proof

HER NEXT-DOOR NEIGHBOUR ran a brothel out of his house when she was living out west. He worked in a bar, and she had just started there as a bartender. This guy had a wife, a lot of tattoos, and loved to party. He would pester Nancy to come and party with him on Friday nights. One night after work, she told a coworker that she was going to go, and he told her what was really happening at the house. She had no interest in that. Not at the time anyway. She was nineteen. Once she got older, "more practical and pragmatic about money," she looked at it a little differently. When she entered her thirties as a divorced woman living back in St. John's, she reflected on her time in industrial work.

Back then she didn't get paid for sex or to perform oral sex, but there was an unspoken expectation. She believed in the theory that oil-patch contractors hired the best looking women with the secret hope they will perform certain off-record duties. That was twenty years ago. It didn't fit her then. She was young, naive, connected to her body in a different way than she is now: a divorced mother of two, who had life experience, had travelled the world, and a fierce independent backbone holding her up. At this point she could separate work from personal.

When times were tough one Christmas and her ex wasn't paying his previously agreed upon amount, she called a downtown massage parlour and asked if they were hiring. It was the easiest money she ever made. Her first client looked like Shaggy from Scooby Doo, a nickname he never lost.

> He was a good sport about it. It was hilarious. I was really nervous, but he didn't even care. I told him it was my first time, and he was like, "No sweat." I was probably only in there for ten minutes, and it was supposed to take a half hour, but I was so nervous. I was shaking and probably acting ridiculously, but he was super happy with it. I didn't feel very confident about myself at the time. I'm a different person now.

Nancy remembers the jaw-dropping feeling of the first time she made $1200 a week. She could support her kids. She could pay her bills. She could buy something for herself for the first time in years. She was finally independent.

> My confidence level went from frumpy, and feeling old and tired, to this fabulous bitch with an I-don't-give-a-fuck-about-what-anybody-says attitude. I feel very strong and empowered and I'm in charge when I'm in that room with a client. They're not in charge of anything. I don't know anyone who feels like they're being taken advantage of, not in our section of the business anyway. We do it because we think it's a smart thing to do. It's such easy money.

So easy, in fact, Nancy and her friends decided to go into business together. She decided to open up her own massage parlour—a sensual massage parlour with an educated feminist at the helm.

Before that though, she worked like the rest of the girls. The owner they worked for had a drug problem and didn't do a great job of keeping the place clean and maintained. "It was seedy and skeety and dirty. We had to fight for cleaning products and toilet paper and towels. It was just horrible."

The workers at the time joked around about owning their own place, the same way many joke about what they'd do if they won the lottery. A little later, the place was shut down but reopened a few months later under new ownership. It quickly regained the rumour of its seedy nature. The older male owner would supply drugs to addicts in exchange for sexual favours. He was rumoured to enjoy having people in his employ who were not in their right mind. Nancy could not stand for that "terrible, terrible stuff." She wanted a place that was clean and safe for all involved. She found it. It was twice as much to rent, which upped the ante on the finances as well as the standards of the girls and the clients. It was a no brainer.

I was a little nervous when Nancy arranged for a tour of the house. Never had I stepped foot in a massage parlour of any kind. I was instructed to take my shoes off and leave them on the mat before entering. It smelled of Febreze, coconut tanning lotion, and lilacs. Each room was equipped with a massage bed as well as a full bathroom with white linens. The old but well-kept house had the original crown mouldings, high ceilings, and dark wood on the stairs and floors. The two lone workers in the lounging area were looking at their phones and sipping Tim's coffees when I was introduced as a friend of the owner. They didn't seem to mind that I was there, but it was obvious that they were reluctant to chat. At the time of the interview, there were eight workers. Because of the nature of the job, they come and go depending on what's going on in their lives. Sometimes someone they know from their "other" life will come in and everyone feels embarrassed. Some girls quit.

> We always say that they're the ones that need to be embarrassed because they're the ones that are coming to us. We're just making a smart business choice. They're just pissing their money away. That's great. We love that. Come in and see us. We don't really feel embarrassed about it. Not to the extent that the clients would be. I don't really see it as a big deal. I've been at it for so long. To me it's just some fun. You get to know somebody and you have a laugh and it's not a relationship type of thing. As a single parent you don't really want to

be getting into relationships anyway. You just want to have a bit of fun and walk away. It's just so not a big deal in so many places, and for people to go and just talk about it in such hushed tones, I mean it's been around longer than any other job. We are recession proof.

The women who work there are supposed to be drug free and appear confident, most are moms trying to provide for their children without being reliant on an ex-husband. Many women, after divorce, particularly if they were not the breadwinners of their home, feel stifling pressure to keep their children's lives the same, which can sometimes mean buying expensive hockey gear, paying for school trips, supplying the latest iPhones, etc. This is not something they ever saw themselves doing, but this work seemed to be a lucrative option that could help them maintain their quality of life.

Having to keep asking an ex for money is really demeaning. It's horrible. I need to make money on my own. I didn't before because I was busy being pregnant and raising kids. It's so much nicer when we can come in and make some money and not have to be begging for money for Christmas gifts or whatever. I do three shifts a week and I can pay for my bills. It's empowering.

One of the most recent surprising patterns is the influx of female customers. Men are the norm, but now they're getting couples and sometimes women alone. Whether it's the clean atmosphere or the safe environment, this is something Nancy never saw before.

We still don't have our minds completely wrapped around it. We try to figure out what they want because, a lot of times, women won't exactly tell you what they want when they come in. We're trying to figure it out as we go along, but once a woman came in on her own and saw somebody and then she brought her husband

back the next time. So that was interesting. Now they're
regular clients.

That becomes a new type of service, one that likely points to an
improvement in their sex life as well as their marriage. There are
a few single women that come in, who are the hardest clients to
decipher.

It is more of a complicated session when you're with a
woman because you don't know what they want, but
when you're with a guy, it's so simple. You know exactly
what they want. You can figure it out just by watching
where their eyes go. With women you just don't know.

The fact that women are coming in means it's upscale. Women
generally do not go to seedy, scary, tacky places for sexual fulfillment.

There seems to be something a little more trustworthy about having
a woman running the show at this massage parlour. As a woman, I
would assume female clients would feel safer, would trust the
establishment a little more by virtue of shared perspectives, fears,
and experiences that women in general face and contemplate that
men likely wouldn't even consider. The trust spans through the
family of workers. For example, the other night a worker refused to
see a customer because he was rough with her the week before—
he smacked her ass without consent—and he was told he had one
more chance and, if he didn't smarten up, they would refuse him
service for good. He chose to leave. That the owner is a woman who
is behind the workers and maintains a clean establishment, makes a
big difference to all involved.

The women seek work there via email. Sometimes Nancy will have
to post ads, but only rarely. It's difficult spreading the word about
jobs of this nature to the general population. "People just don't see
it as something that they should do." The stigma around it is partly
attributed to the lack of knowledge about the different types of work
people are doing.[62]

---

62 This is called whore stigma.

The experience can be intimate, and while some might think this behavior is deviant or promotes violence, that is not necessarily so. For instance, there is a code for the workers if they're in trouble— they stomp on the floor and whoever's in the house will come running. They've never had to use it.

Nancy believes those responsible for Bill C-36 have a narrow-minded view of the reality of sex work.

> I feel like the people that wrote that bill just don't have a clue. They're seriously right-wing, religious conservatives that sit in judgement of everyone around them. Who are they that they can decide what's moral for other people? Just because they don't want to do it, what does that have to do with everybody else? The men that are writing these laws, I guess they're not doing it, or they're doing it from such high-priced places that they think they'll never get caught.[63]

She does not believe that sex is a sacred act, an opinion that she did not have even ten years ago.

> If you wanna go have sex, just go have sex with some-body. It's just a silly, innocuous thing. That's why I don't understand marriage. It's so boring. I have all of those understandings now that I probably didn't have until I was in my thirties. I might have thought about it, but I couldn't really define it. I know myself more now. I just don't see sex as a big deal. We women grow up emulating princesses and can't wait to get married, and we have sex for the first time and it's such a big deal, but really it's not. It astonishes me that the Canadian government thinks it's going to solve all these problems with C-36. Conservative politicians think that every hooker has a needle in her arm and that's not the way it

---

63 From talking to various organizations about how law-enforcement agencies treat and deal with individuals selling sex from the street, as well as local massage parlours, the consensus is that workers are usually left alone until residents complain, there are rumours of underage girls around, or someone reports being victimized.

is. The bigger problem is a lot of these politicians are women. They don't want their husbands coming to see us. Most women are going to be anti sex work. It's really hard to find a feminist, smart, drug-free, responsible person that says, "I can do this." It's harder to find a feminist, smart, drug-free, responsible politician that will support us. People think it's all around bad, and it can be so different than that. It really bothers me that a lot of people would look at me and say, "Oh my god, she's a dirty whore" kinda thing.

Nancy exhales. "Maybe I am if you compare what they're willing to do—missionary-style sex every Saturday night for the rest of their lives."

The argument comes down to the nature of morality when money is involved. One of the girls at the house recently admitted, "I do less here for money than I would do for free when I was just one drink over on a Friday night on George." Nancy alludes to the fact that most restaurants hire gorgeous, young women who wear tight, revealing clothing to serve patrons.

Like cocktail waitressing in a bar, when someone grabs your ass and you get mad at them, the boss is not happy with you. If someone is grabbing your ass and tipping you and buying drinks, you're supposed to shut up and take it. I've had lots of jobs like that before. Sometimes it's the owners too. The managers are always so full of themselves. I'm so sick of jobs like that.

At least here, everything's up front—cash and intentions.

Most clients are good—they pay and act accordingly—but there are a few clients who get upset from time to time. One reason could be that their favourite girl moved on and they lack the nerve to see someone else. It's happened a handful of times that someone Nancy knows in her personal life has come in looking for services, which can go either way: they have a laugh and proceed as normal, or the guy feels too awkward and leaves.

Recently, a man kept calling; let's call him Creepy Tim. He's rumoured to be not only creepy, but also disease ridden.

> He calls every day, calls every service provider in town every day just to talk. I guess he doesn't have anything else to do, but no one will see him anymore here. I think they might see him in other places. He gets off on knowing people's personal details. He wants to know their real names, what they do, where they live. It's super creepy. We won't see him anymore, but he still calls every day and asks who's working. He must be keeping a list or something.

This sort of sex-addict compulsion is outside the norm. Most clients are exactly what one would expect. Nancy estimates at least fifty percent are married. Men with money wearing suits and overcoats are the ideal clients because, if they get good service, they will return. For many of the women who work in this industry, contacts can be made for professional services in all areas: legal, accounting, financial planning, banking, government, education, industry, entertainment, sports, business. "We see all kinds."

It's rare, but in the past they have gotten unwelcome guests such as a mother of one of the workers, who showed up unannounced at the door. She was on some kind of medication, and because of her erratic behaviour, they could not let her in the building. Sometimes girl/boyfriends or spouses discover where their girlfriend or partner works, and that can be stressful for all involved. Nancy always suggests that workers speak to their partners about the work they are doing, but not all are in a position to do so. The workers protect each other as best they can with emergency contact information and offering places to stay if things go awry. One girl was beaten up and hospitalized by her boyfriend when he found out. She left the business and kept the boyfriend in spite of all the support she was offered by her coworkers. Nancy feels sad but sighs and says, "You can't win them all."

The police have been called once. A client called the police because he wanted a refund. The girl kicked him out with ten minutes left because he pinned her down. He did it once. She told him he couldn't do it. He did it again. She told him to get out. "It's few and far between that women are willing to be submissive in these rooms." After persisting and then realizing he wasn't going to get his money back, he got fed up and called the police. Needless to say, they did not enforce the refund. However, the officers suggested that the women close up for the night because the client refused to leave. He adamantly remained sitting in his car in front of the house, making the women feel ill-at-ease.[64]

One time, a drunk was out on the back step at 3am sending pictures via email. He did not realize that they had been closed for three hours and there was no one there.[65] Drunks are the people Nancy strives to avoid, hence the early closing time and permission to refuse service to anyone who seems over their limit. It's not just that people under the influence can pass out or vomit or get unruly, according to Nancy, it also feels a little shady taking money from someone who might not remember what happened in the morning and think he was ripped off.

Sometimes people park outside to see who's coming in and out. Nancy brushes it off as people just wanting to amuse themselves for a while. No one has ever threatened them with photos of clients or made clients feel uncomfortable, except for reporters filming once when a city politician made news of them. The filming and reporting was shut down within a few hours after a call to a women's group in the city.

The spouse of a patron contacted the house once, curious about credit-card billings:

> She started looking at the numbers on his cellphone, and called saying, "What is this place?"—we save all

---

64 Since this incident (not because of the incident, but to constructively deal with situations like this), RNC officers are now receiving sensitivity training to better handle disagreements involving sex work and sex workers.

65 Nancy has received many pictures of male genitalia. She doesn't understand why men insist on sending these pictures because it's not anything they care to see.

the numbers so the girls know who's calling—and the girls would just ask if she'd like to make an appointment. She found out eventually and he was grounded. We didn't see him for six months. He just came back last week or the week before, and now he makes a point of using a different name, so I don't know if he figures his wife won't be able to find him if he's using a different name, but we still know who he is.

Another client who was caught by his wife now only calls from pay phones or other public lines. They have saved his information in several different numbers that he frequently uses, but it doesn't matter because the workers know everyone by voice after a short time anyway.

People who pay for anything via PayPal should know that street addresses and real names are all made available to the payee. Nancy has invoices with all of that information, although she maintains that she will never share them. Maybe some people just aren't afraid to get caught or have no one who could catch them. Some clients just come in and swipe their cards matter-of-factly and without any embarrassment. Often there are emails that go back and forth prior to a first appointment where "menu items" are discussed. Clients can prepay for the services of their choosing. Their low inhibitions might be due to the excitement leading up to the visit or it could be that they don't see the transaction as a big deal.

Nancy's establishment has hired a bouncer who is also a dominatrix.

She's done self-defense classes, and she can actually tackle people. We've had health-care professionals, social-services professionals, tutors, educators, and a bunch of crazy people all working together. It's a fun place to be. Because of the job we do, it's just so funny, the conversations that we have are ridiculous and hilarious.

While there's a lot of fun and games, it's obviously far from perfect, mostly due to the current status of law around sex work and owning a bawdy house. Nancy's dream is to have an establishment where the girls can have cards that say, *Nancy has been tested and is free of certain diseases by such and such a date.* They do this in some places in British Columbia. Right now that is impossible in St. John's.

> We just want to be at that level. We want to get rid of all the seediness. Most of us are smart, easy-going women. We [St. John's] need places like this. I try to say to people, you want this. You don't want a picture of the city in the newspaper where people are saying someone was found at the dump.

Nancy and many others feel that stigmatizing laws that penalize sex workers and clients make that a less possible reality. Nancy says that while her place was closed down due to a permitting issue a while back, two working women were assaulted in separate incidents in upscale hotels in St. John's. Neither were willing to press charges because of the fear of being outed. Maybe the assaults couldn't have been prevented. But maybe, Nancy insists, if women could press charges using their work names, those men wouldn't have gotten away with it.

> I really hate it when the women say they feel like something's wrong with them. I tell them they're smart. This is an independence plan. A divorce plan. Even if it just allows us a place to work for a little while. I could walk into a minimum job right now, and with this in addition to that, I'll make good money. I'll be able to take care of myself and my kids.

"Most people don't think they'd ever do it, but everyone has a price."

Dragon Presence

CHELSEA MET ME AT the door of the Cotton Club on a sub-zero January night dressed in eight-inch platform stilettos, a black G-string with hip clips, a matching top that had slits across the breast pockets, a high-waisted lace slip, and a custom-made, short, green and gold kimono inspired by her memorable experiences with Asian clientele. She was smiling. Her curly blond hair danced around her back.

We made our way through the club and up the steps to the private dancing area. Brown booths lined the wall and we got cozy on a black love seat. She plugged in her phone—she needed a charge and her "beats"—and we settled in to chat.

She takes issue with the sex-worker label. She does not consider herself a sex worker. She does not exchange intercourse for money. She is an adult entertainer who is participating in the research because she feels it's important for people to know the realities of the stripper lifestyle, realities that can ruin one's life if they're not careful. She's a dancer, was one since she was a kid in dance lessons. She reminisces that the first time she stripped it was like a weird jazz routine.

She's thirty-four, but under the dim light of the club, she looks ten years younger. "For the most part, I made all the right choices." Thirty-four is old to be dancing on stage and being successful at it, but Chelsea is a pro[66]. Her first time in front of the crowd was the August before she turned seventeen. She had a two-year-old daughter at home, couldn't find daycare and didn't want to be on social assistance.

New to Newfoundland, she came in search of good people and a clean club. On the mainland there was a lot of "extras" happening around her that she did not like such as "blow jobs and hand jobs" and she couldn't stand being around it. She wasn't cut out for it. She wanted to dance. That was it. Her stage presence and her verbal communication with the customers between shows in the bar were usually enough to capture them. She didn't want to foray into prostitution. A patron who knew her well saw it and said, "You don't fucking belong here."

"I haven't belonged anywhere for a really long time."

He gave her some money and told her "to go book the damn ticket to St. John's." Once she reached her destination—Newfoundland—she earned some clean cash and sent him $200 to say thank you, and he replied with, "Fuck off, kiddo! Now go create a new life for yourself." A year and a half later, she is still here.

Having worked in Newfoundland for a while now, she knows the lay of the land and feels quite comfortable. While she has strong lines for herself, not everyone appreciates those same lines or rules. So Chelsea keeps her head down, and doesn't necessarily engage with anyone who looks her way, something she has learned as a survival strategy throughout her time spent at dozens of clubs across the mainland. "It's not like the mainland clubs out here." She compares St. John's to Chuck E. Cheese. Child's play. She values the constant tourism and the turnover of the girls.

But conflict still finds her at times, mostly when people are drinking and tempers are high. She can be somewhat sheepish in these

---

66 Older than thirty-four is old in general for anyone working in the sex industry. It is obviously an industry based on youth and looks, and the illusion of youth gets harder to maintain once you get to your thirties. Women often lie about their age if they're older than thirty-five. The younger they are, or claim to be, the more money they potentially make.

situations leaving others to assume that she's not fierce inside. She prefers her colleagues to consider her of no importance, a defensive strategy acquired through her experiences, but when she's onstage her strength shows and the other girls don't like it. "Who does she think she is?" is often being whispered around the room, something she can feel even while performing. One girl accused her of "auditioning for Broadway."

The "vibe" in many strip clubs is often palpable. There's the good, the bad, the cliché, and the surprising. Some girls are independent and fierce, others are pimped. "Some of them are pimping each other, some pimps are getting girls straight from suburban parks." She's tried to help people if she thought they wanted help. "They used to call me Captain Save a Ho because I would want to help everyone." She was even once confronted by a pimp with a gun while sitting in her drop top after a long night's work. Earlier that night, she had agreed to help one of the girls get out of town and figure her life out. After that incident, she knew she had to stop caring and just do her own thing.

Pimps are hard to pinpoint in St. John's. Do they exist? Where are they? How powerful are they? Are they related to larger organized crime units? Chelsea says there are indeed pimps who operate downtown, but they're not overt. It's nowhere near the presence that exists in other bigger cities across Canada. She goes on to explain that some of the pimps operate in large groups that include family members populated by fifth and sixth generation pimps. "They grow up in the game. It's normal for them. I feel sad that they haven't seen another way of life. When they get a new girl they refer to her grooming as bumping a bitch. They make her part of the team, make her feel special." Sometimes this involves intimidation, consensual or forced sex work, mostly from hotels. It normally originates in a slow grooming process that revolves around alcohol and drugs.

Chelsea feels that people should leave "The Rock" alone. "This is our rock, get the fuck out of here, you mainlanders." On one occasion, there was a large group of pimps dominating the club's main floor, which was intimidating for customers. The presence of perceived pimps can run through the room in moments. Apparently, they come and watch the girls, look for girls who are free agents. It's not anything new to Chelsea and she never wants to be a part of it. Being around it makes her depressed, but she can cope with it. She's desensitized to it, but she hates seeing these young women make choices that could negatively impact their lives in large and long-term ways.

Chelsea's save-a-ho mentality has largely been reserved for younger girls who don't know what they're getting into yet. All they know is they want to make some real money.

> They typically get pregnant young and they want to be independent. They see prostitution as an easy access point to power, power that they've never had. Power that they see and hear about on music videos. They have no idea what's going to happen to them. I don't think they even notice for the first couple of years. They start to realize how bad it could get depending on the boyfriend or the pimp's attitude. They act like they're putting up with you stripping, that you should be lucky for them to be attracted to you knowing that you're selling your body, you're getting all this attention from men and the boyfriend/pimp puts up with it. You're lucky that he's fucking you or at least that's what your groomed into believing. So I would love for girls at least in St. John's to know that you can be a clean dancer and be very proud, be very empowered, file your taxes, don't do drugs, invest, don't let anyone be mean to you, and have a wonderful life. I've watched so many girls be destroyed, wither away to nothing. They call me up decades later and tell me they wish they had listened to me. Some of them suffer from really scary abuse and diseases.

She goes on to mention some personal conversations she's had with people who suffered through ovarian cancer or some other potentially fatal diseases.

"I'm a feminist. I want to help. Girl power. But I'm not going to waste time trying to help someone if they don't want it. I need to help myself."

Stripping and other forms of sex work have a tumultuous relationship with feminism.[67] The perspectives can be severely divided. If I'm considering only my own personal feminism, I believe that women should have total control over their bodies, that no other individual or government should have the power to restrict their freedom of choice. Many feminists would vehemently disagree on the nature of that freedom in regards to sex work, believing that stripping is a long-time result of patriarchal control. Chelsea finds stripping "empowering." The big problem she identifies now is that, "There's nobody monitoring the clubs, and the girls aren't being taught anything. There's no leaders anymore. Girls need women to emulate."[68] Because Chelsea has been around for longer than many of the other girls she works with, she feels a lot has been lost. "When I started, all the girls were like me, and you were the minority to be selling sex. You were the minority to have a boyfriend, a title most pimps hide behind." This empowered attitude does not necessarily serve Chelsea well among other dancers. She feels ostracized much of the time. "People are like, what's with this chick? I'm just totally being myself."

She defines herself as an anomaly in that she's smart and eloquent and tries to contradict the idea that because she dances for money she's stupid or has nothing else going for her. She explains that,

---

67 According to *Sex Workers in the Maritimes Talk Back,* most feminist theory has focused on the sex worker as victim. "Radical feminists [. . .] insist on a feminism that renders sex workers passive victims. This type of feminism locates the sex worker body in a totalizing patriarchy, one that blames men for exploiting women's sexuality. Sex workers are victims and, therefore, unable to act or negotiate sex acts for themselves" (9).

68 Chelsea's views on stripping harken back to when stripping began in the late 1800s in the form of burlesque or theatrical satire. It wasn't until the 1980s that it really changed for what Chelsea would call the worst. It became a free-for-all. At the turn of the twentieth century, the very thing that made strippers so attractive was the fact that they were ultimately untouchable (Van der Meulen, *Selling Sex,* 32).

"Most male customers are much more comfortable with a dancer who appears ignorant; they're paranoid of the judgment an intelligent woman might pass on the purchase of a dance," but she doesn't consider buying lap dances an act of desperation. She herself has enjoyed the service while attending a bar on her off time.

While working, she prefers to be around smart and talented performers who aren't afraid of a little healthy competition.

> I've come to find over the years that a really strong stage show with a clever selection of music can really earn the respect of even the biggest hater. Sometimes I'll play 70s rock 'n' roll, rap, or dance hall (a genre of reggae) all in one night so that the dancers who might be scooting me or trying to figure me out can see that I'm a force to be reckoned with. I dance really strong and sometimes a little crazy.

She uses her music choice wisely. Because her childhood was cut short, she often feels nostalgic about that time and has a soft spot for the music. She chooses stuff not because people may like it but because it will leave an impression.

> So I've come to realize that my stage presence gains a lot of respect from a lot other girls and then the ones who would be the hardest or whatever just back off or eventually come around. Like at first, they hate, but then, even if they still do, they come around and start to show me respect anyway. Initially I hear they think I'm a big-headed Barbie, like fuck that bitch. Everybody always tells me, "You're so full of yourself," "you seemed like such a bitch," "you're a mean girl." All because I'm confident, good at what I do, and keep to myself when I'm new because I know better.

The customers, however, are attracted by her demeanor.

Chelsea prefers customers in the fifty to sixty age range. She sometimes complies with the perception that she's mixed race because the customers debate with her endlessly about her age, race, and real name. If they're fifty-five, and she's a young looking white girl, she's young enough to be their daughter, and the customers do not like that. Fibbing about her race occasionally will end a redundant debate and make her more appealing because ethnically diverse women were rare in the communities these Newfoundland men grew up in. "I can read people from across the room. I can feel people looking at me, and I can tell what they're thinking most of the time. It's not always aggressive perversion." Sometimes, it's just curiosity.

She does meet up with customers outside of the bar. She doesn't consider this doing outcalls. Sometimes they want to go pub hopping, shopping, or greeting clients over expensive dinners. And she's performed graphic lesbian sex shows in the past with her girlfriends. She says she would be doing it anyway, so why not?

> During a show, the customers cellphones are collected and they're instructed that exposing or touching themselves is not allowed. The minute someone pulls some shit, I jump up, pack up everything, and leave because I've already been prepaid. I call conservative people square bears. They'll book a show for their one wild night out. They pick me strategically after getting to know me and realizing my attitude is 100 percent professional show girl. They're happy to have nothing to be ashamed of and could potentially go on to share this experience with their wives. If they're grateful and very appreciative, I'm going to give them a really great show. So as soon as that changes, if any of those aspects change, my attitude spikes right up, I'm mean and cold. I'll leave, and I'll leave with the money.

These private lesbian shows, which are very expensive, are usually only booked for bachelor parties or during big events in major cities across North America. She chooses her clientele wisely to make sure nothing makes her feel uncomfortable. Some of this depends on the body language and information she can ascertain from the exchange in the bar:

> I always dance for them first, and I overly tease them so I can confirm the level of self-control and respect the client's capable of. I'll put myself in positions that push a rude customer to cross lines. Good guys will calmly enjoy any position and not attempt to push my boundaries. Conservative patrons are satisfied just by watching, which is the ideal situation because you get a deep sense of gratitude for your eroticism, and that's the greatest for flattery. Real performers consider it a craft, but we exist in a business that rarely recognizes this talent. People who realize how we feel to be fighting for a creative outlet are the only people I really want to be around. I like a little physical contact, but I'd rather be the one initiating it.

In Chelsea's experience, some of the customers who use cocaine can be quite relaxing to be around—as odd as it sounds.[69] They can easily spend a lot of time and money simply enjoying hilarious conversation. Once they start doing coke, she knows they aren't going to be thinking about erections. "It's fun telling stories and talking about life and having a ball. It's basically like cable TV. They know they're not getting anything but my fucking time. They love it and so do I. It's great."

Many dancers will do extras for money inside and outside of the bar if they can get away with it, such as touching beyond the allotted rules and any sexual exchange you can humanly imagine. Chelsea hazards a guess that the number's around ninety-seven percent. The other three percent might be new to the game or have taken extended periods of time off. "Most of the dancers will grab a guy's dick over the jeans or let the guys suck their tits if they're trying to seal the deal for more dances." Some of them even go as far as to lie about how many songs are owed. Chelsea considers this dumb

---

69 A known side effect of prolonged cocaine use is erectile dysfunction.

business. She has also seen the clubs make the assumption that girls will always work no matter their treatment. In her experience, this diminishes the quality of performers and hurts everyone.

> No matter how vaguely the line has been crossed, I consider this an act of war. It means you're lowering the bar for all of us and creating a space where men expect us to submit, beg, or weasel our way to our earnings. When guys open their mouths to reach for my nipple, they're like a baby bird reaching for food. On several occasions, I've tried to enlighten them by pointing out that any dancer who allows them to do so has most certainty also let every other customer rub their saliva all over her nipple. They're usually like, "I don't care."

She jokes that it took her years to stop being shocked by this response, and that these are probably also the guys that go home with chlamydia. "I don't do that. I consider that crossing the line. I maintain the rules."

It never ceases to amaze Chelsea that some dancers may even decide to forego using a condom for an extra $50 or a gram of coke. "There are plenty of girls who do extras within the club, they organize dates for later, and until the management catches up with them, it's safe to say it's more cost effective to take the week off than to gamble the cost of floor fees. They will eventually be fired, but the cycle will begin all over again week after week. I have to be lucky and catch the good customers between all the nonsense the club tries to keep a handle on."

For the women who foray into more risky behaviour, sometimes the consequences can be irrevocable. Most of the desperate behaviour is attached to money. They turn to drugs and alcohol after feeling abused and used for too long and eventually consider all men to be horrible human beings, and the only way to get around that is to numb themselves with their narcotic of choice. Chelsea realizes that looking down on the customers is a self-preservation mechanism.

If the girls didn't feel so ashamed of their actions, they wouldn't get so caught up in drugs and alcohol. This is where she differentiates herself. She never does drugs and barely drinks: no small feat when the majority of your life is spent in clubs. "I just don't feel bad, so I don't need to numb myself."

Many dancers rely on drugs and alcohol and think it becomes an important part of their hustle, but they lose something in the pursuit of the hustle.

> I call them the by-any-means-necessary girls who are going to do whatever they can to get every last dollar possible because they think the men are all pieces of shit. That's not my mentality. Never has been. Never will be, I don't let people do anything I don't like. Even when I'm broke. I'm just broke. I live by a line from the movie *The Player's Club*, which is "Make the money. Don't let it make you." I prance around being my happy self. I run around the bar, chatting people up and having fun. I like to consider myself a farmer, planting seeds all throughout the night.

This approach has worked well in the pursuit of acquiring long-term customers.

> I don't conform or play a role to sell a dance. Sometimes I'll play along as I've said, but it's normally only to stop a lengthy repetitious conversation. Depending on the tact, experience, or caliber of the man I've encountered, I can be perceived as uptight and not fun at all or incredibly talented and totally exciting. I can make some money doing what I'm extremely comfortable doing, which is being a little physical and passionate because I just naturally am. If they don't press my boundaries or show disrespect, I'll make some money and they feel good about it. If they give me attitude, act pushy or demanding, I'll walk out

minus any amount of money owing just to make a statement. On a good night, I can walk out with $600. It all depends on the type of people that are here. You never know what to expect. There's no real good day of the week. Some Mondays can be fabulous, and some Fridays can be terrible. If someone's in town on an unexpected overnight they'll normally have the attitude that they're stuck here for a night, I'll enjoy telling them stories about life on the island and seducing them into wanting to come back. They won't have any problem spending money on a hot girl at the strip club. They're often surprised to hear how wonderful my life is here.

The most important thing for Chelsea is that stripping has enabled her to raise her daughter alone. "How many moms get to read their kids a bedtime story every night and be there when they get up in the morning without ever using childcare? She recalls her six-year-old daughter saying, "Mommy, I wish we could make wishes on stars and then they would turn into presents." She tears up relaying this to me.

Being a mom and a dancer is what her life is based on, which includes breaking the stigma of being a dancer and a teenage mom. These are her main drivers. "I successfully hid this from her for her whole life even though many individuals close to me still continue to reprimand me for not being honest. Throughout all of her life I've always known when the right time for each age was, so I'm going to continue to listen to my gut and trust my instincts."

Although sometimes it wasn't easy to stay true to her convictions when faced with years of being a young single mom, she persevered. The women around her were making large amounts of money, and she had ample opportunity to prostitute herself to make more. There were dark moments when she contemplated it, but she decided not to get into that life. She didn't want to lose sight of herself and saw what it was doing to the women around her.

Using her mother as an example, she was able to stick to her plan of not crossing her own moral lines.

> My mom was a really powerful business woman. You know if I was raised by a different woman I might not have had that strong, independent, female attitude. Once you realize that guys are lucky to be in your presence, your standards go up. I was able to realize that these men were lucky to share my thoughts, time and touch. You're lucky to enjoy my body that I work so hard on. I don't feel that I need to do whatever the client wants, nor do their inquiries insult me if they respect my opinion, which majority of the time they do.

She also feels that her sexuality plays a part in this discipline. She describes it as being a little more fluid than some women.

> Maybe you're more heterosexual than I could ever be, so maybe you really love cock all the time. Maybe you want to take your cock all day long. I know a lot of girls who like that, who don't even charge for it. It's all fine and dandy, but once it turns into something you have to do, you start hating yourself. You start making a lot of other choices you don't realize you're making, and you turn into a piece of shit and so does your life and so does everybody around you. It just spirals out of control.

She likens it to a regular work situation where you may lose sight of your own values to get ahead, like throwing your coworkers under the bus or brown nosing your way to the top. Many of the girls resort to prescription drugs, alcohol, and street drugs to cope with the consequences of these choices.

Chelsea had a brief struggle with addiction when she was younger, a behaviour she feels is still affecting her cognitive abilities today. She blames it on the desperation to fit in and make friends or to stop feeling emotional pain. She was sixteen at the time, and a customer who also sold cocaine kept bugging her to "get with him." He intimidated her by telling her he knew she was underage, and because she was so desperate to remain off government assistance, she agreed to play the role of "his old lady." He would slide $100 bills at her across the table and then just let her go on her way. Privately there was no physical relationship between them, but he promised her a car if she cleaned up and got her beginner's license. She ended up quitting because she wanted her license and her car, and she had no other means to get it. She got clean pretty fast. He kept his word and eventually set her up in a much nicer club and rental property.

Even though she was a child at the time, that fire was already in her. She knew what she wanted and went after it. While attractive and striking, she doesn't think that's the reason she has managed this far. "I always had a good aura around me. It is the sweetness in my soul that people kind of want to get a taste of." It's also her confidence. It's obvious when you meet her that she is a vibrant, confident woman. She is the type of woman you want to be around on a regular basis because she's full of life.

The other dancers don't always agree. She handles most of it with ease, and is close to some of them, but she's fully aware that negativity can swarm around her. She also can't condone if a woman is allowing herself to be abused or is giving her money away. "I can't handle it. I can't be your friend. I'll try to lead you down the right path when you're interested but I can't deal with insanity. I feel like I'll lose pieces of me being around that shit." She has mastered the art of letting go of people who only take away from her life.

> Even if you've said and done some horrible things, but you're wanting something different and you want to be around me to get inspired. I'm open to that. I'm always open to that, but I won't go out of my way to try to convince girls to change their lives anymore. They're going to turn around and tell their man everything I said, so I'll be very careful and keep my distance these days. It really breaks my heart though. I have to watch

them wasting their lives all around me and I can't do anything about it. It's really hard and often painful for me.

Unfortunately, she has to think about this—the opinions, power, and actions of the boyfriends or the retaliation of whoever benefits from the drug purchasing—when she's making friends with other women at the bar, and she has no time for that nonsense.

She also has no time for disrespectful DJs. The dynamics between a DJ and a dancer are powerful. The DJ's voice can reverberate throughout the club. "It sets the tone and dictates to the patrons how they can treat the girls." For instance, if you have a DJ who loves his job and is passionate about the success of the bar, much like in any workplace, the experience for everyone involved is good. On the other side, if you have a DJ who is negative, hostile, and confrontational, who doesn't care about the work or the girls, and is drained of passion, he can affect the girls on a deep-rooted level. Chelsea's witnessed dancers engage in drug abuse due to negative, abusive, or unethical treatment from the DJ. If the relationship between the dancers and their DJ is strong, the bar is packed and it's too busy to abuse a lot of drugs or alcohol, for that matter. "Hence the word *hustle*.[70] Move your ass. The club is packed and there's line ups to get dances."

She also has no time for customers disrespecting her in the bar. She finds it's not usually a problem because with her firm actions she teaches people how to treat her, something she attributes to her "dragon presence," something she's only really embraced in her thirties.

When she was younger, men tried to manipulate her by telling her she had beautiful eyes while trying to reach for her vagina. She wasn't confident then and they would try and push her around.

---

70 There's a reason why it's called a hustle: strippers are constantly trying to persuade customers to spend their money. According to *Sex Workers Unite: A History of the Movement from Stonewall to Slutwalk,* this is called "performativity" and is "similar to the work performed by other 'smiling' occupations" (134).

If the guys think that you don't respect yourself and you have a shitty life, they're likely to assume they can get away with anything and that you also likely give your money away. They don't fucking care. They use it against you as a tool to pressure you. I've now made it my personal mission to teach all the men how to treat us. It doesn't seem like anybody else is going to, and something needs to be done about it.

Chelsea finds her no-holds-barred attitude helps her acquire long-term clients. She's been approached in the change rooms many times by girls and staff who tell her she needs to hustle. Sometimes they mock her.

Okay, babe, like you're the same age as my daughter and you're going to come teach me about my hustle? Often it's a guy teaching them the aggressive hustle, but I come from a different time and my strategy is a lot more intellectual than that. We should be learning from each other, not guys. At the end of the day, people need camaraderie. They need a team because you can get ahead faster as a unit. Do I want to be in a team with other girls where we could all pitch on groceries, eat like kings, share fitness and buy properties? Fuck yeah. Why do we need a man to figure that out? We're all so segregated and divided amongst ourselves. It prevents us from forming genuine bonds and long-term relationships that could in turn really empower us. So I have been on a bit of a mission over the last year or so, to somehow align that. That's what I hope in the end. I see myself retiring around a group of strong, intelligent, brilliant performers.

This is her dream. After spending twenty years in the adult-entertainment industry, she keeps that dream alive even though her experience with people has told her otherwise. She could write a book on what she's learned about other people as well as herself, such as where her lines are in terms of what she's willing to do or not do to fit in. She can quickly see and decide if someone or some action will add to her life experience, whether it be sexually or professionally. She's learned that time alone thinking and dreaming is good, which gives her new drive to connect with people, to have a clear conscience in her work, to do her best job at all times.

Because she's so driven and dedicated to dancing, personal relationships with men have been somewhat difficult to maintain.

> It's hard to find a guy who truly trusts and believes that I'm not doing more, and even if he does, the contact I have with other men is still upsetting for them. I've realized lately that I'm polyamorous—a term that resonates with me to my core—and most men are not aligned with that. Eventually, what I'm comfortable with physically makes him feel like less of a man because why should anybody else be able to touch me?

In her experience, men will act okay with her stripping in the beginning, but eventually, when their feelings for her develop, they can't happily cope anymore. They get upset that she expects them to support her love for her work, and once again she feels compelled to conform to keep her love interest content.

> Then there's the guys who are so sexual and so what-ever that they get off on hearing about it. It's like a fetish to them, but they're more like the kind of guy I want to enjoy for a short time, not really the type I would contemplate sharing a life with. You can never really get the whole package.

In her younger days she was with one man who harped on her a lot. He preached the notion that no one loved her and stripping was the only way for her to get attention.

> It took me many years to find myself and be able to identify that I feel great about myself naked because that's the way I was raised. I wasn't raised to believe that

nudity was sin. I don't have a religious family. Because I didn't grow up ashamed of myself, I had a lot of self-love. I don't carry the shame people expect me to carry. So don't head fuck me. When you're young and impressionable, you start to believe it's true. He loves me, he's telling me the truth, and even with my strong will and my knowhow, I would still be convinced by people like that. I would think this is all I'm worth and what am I doing with my life? Why? Because I couldn't command any happiness in my own sex life outside of work, I would isolate myself, become really depressed and lonely. It felt like all I would do was give all these older men a great day. Then when I got off work, I had nothing to fulfill myself. I didn't have passion, and I hadn't established my own true sexuality yet. Once I was able to do that and realize where I was lacking, I was able to feel happy.

Finding a romantic partner who understands this mindset is nearly impossible. Chelsea does not believe you should have to sacrifice an ounce of who you are for someone else. As a dancer, your focus is always on others: the patrons need to like you, the other dancers need to like you, the bar staff needs to like you. "In this industry, you just fall apart because all you're ever doing is for everyone else. When you get off work, you're sacrificing for that person, male or female or whatever, and at the end of the day, you're stripped away. There's nothing left of yourself." It takes a strong sense of self to stay healthy in this kind of environment that at its most simplistic is about physical appearance, but ends up having deep mental and emotional consequences.

Chelsea feels that to understand all of these layers you need to have depth, but such depth can also be your enemy. Ignorance is surely bliss when it comes to navigating the various emotions and existential questions and feminist arguments that come with stripping, which is why she has not told her daughter about her life in the clubs.

Why would I tell her at the wrong time, make her question her entire childhood and think and wonder about what else I've lied about? All that's going to do to her is make her head spin and make her not focus on these difficult aspirations at her age, right? I wanted her to think that we struggled growing up because of how young I was when I had her. I want her to know about everything, but not yet. I don't feel confident that she'll believe who I've been all these years. If she knew that I was doing this and didn't believe and support that, it would make me not respect her. That would break our partnership and our love. I don't want that to happen. One day she's probably going to find out. I'm going to have to sit down and tell her all the things that I'm telling you. Do I want to do that to a young girl's mind, who isn't chasing that life? Why would I want to do that? It's going to put a negative cloud on being a woman in her life, and it's sad because of the stigma and all the misconceptions in the industry.

If the industry cleaned up and went back to a more respectable culture, Chelsea could get behind it.

I would love to tell her my story, but I don't have much faith in anybody doing what needs to be done in the industry to change things. There should be policies. You should need to, as a dancer, get a license. I think there should always be an audition. If you can't audition in person, I think you should be required to send a video. I think your stage presence should be questioned, the way you move, the way you dress should be questioned, the way you speak to customers should be questioned. It should be an interview, and then the people who are interviewing you, I think, should be well-versed in what makes an amazing entertainer.

The stage show should be about talent. Chelsea can dance in eight-inch heels. I get dizzy just thinking about that. She prefers to be in bare feet or in spikes.

> I dance really fast and I run around and tip toe and I leap and I do silly stuff. I entertain. Nowadays a lot of girls move like zombie robots. I think they're trying to hypnotize the guys, I'm not sure, but a lot of customers complain to me about it. Like if Ester Canadas was doing the zombie robot, would I get hypnotized? For like a minute maybe, but it's going to get boring if not awkward. We're only on stage for seven minutes at a time, so even if I'm a really drunk man, I'm pretty sure I would be bored of this a few minutes in. I'd much rather see a girl let go and even look a bit foolish trying to put on a show than watch a girl take stage who has absolutely zero love of the trade. That's exactly what stripping is. Dancing is a skilled trade with or without clothes.

There are a handful of dancers in Canada who are like pro-athletes. They have zero toxic habits, treat their bodies like temples, and make $10,000 a night. That takes will, self-respect, and determination, and those qualities are few and far between.

Chelsea thinks of dancing as fitness. In order to give the best stage show possible, working out is part of her lifestyle. "I have a cross trainer at my house. I drink about thirty waters every day. And not too cold, around room temperature, so that I can drink a lot more. It's a habit for me." She doesn't eat wheat, refined sugar, or drink alcohol regularly. At the time of the interview, she was on a three-week detox. She does thirty minutes of cross training every day. Every time she walks by her stove, she does five chin ups. She will practice her routine with the kettle bell, so when she gets on stage, she feels weightless. Gyms are not her thing; although she does go to the gym sometimes. She feels the various gazes in different ways, and this makes her feel uncomfortable.

I try to go to the gym but I get a bit arrogant when it comes to being paid for people to look at me. So when I'm at the gym and I feel people staring at me, I don't like it. Some girls come up to me and say, "You're really pretty," but girls do that. Men are just trying to figure out if I strip. They wonder if I'm married. Older women want to keep their boyfriends close when they walk by, they switch where they're standing. They pull their shirts down to show their own cleavage. Moms with babies kind of look at me like, "My gosh you're so fun and vibrant." I'm usually on the phone. I play music out loud everywhere I go. At times I'm very loud and obnoxious, and some girls cringe. I mean, not every single person, but it's fluid throughout my day. I just like to be happy me, what can I say.

In Chelsea's mind, the negative treatment is a result of women not supporting each other, and as a feminist, Chelsea is very much in support of other women. In fact, she thinks most women do not use their power properly if at all. After talking to Chelsea for an hour, it's obvious that she is a strong, independent thinker who is not afraid to voice her opinions about gender politics.

I think men dominate our emotions, they dominate our bodies, they dominate our finances. I also feel that, at every moment, I'm that woman that guys joke about how women have it so easy and that pretty women get whatever the fuck they want. That's some bullshit. In my opinion, many wives play the role of a full-time, long-term prostitute. The majority of the time I'm just scraping by trying to survive while not conforming to this. So when I can be a big bad man-killing machine, I do it, and maybe I get referred to as man-hater, but I don't particularly agree with it at all.

A feminist? Yes. A man-hater? No.[71] Feminism is an important part

---

71 Some people think feminism and misandry are synonymous, but any educated feminist will tell you otherwise. Women who bash men are just as sexist as men who bash women. Feminism is about empowering women in various ways, not man-hating.

of what Chelsea does. She feels there should be more of it in the culture of stripping. "The thing is that strip clubs fifteen-plus years ago were gentlemen clubs—there was some class. It was an adult environment. Our society is changing."

Her opinion is that strip clubs are the epitome of humanity.

> I keep a lot of marriages healthy and happy. I do a lot of psychology verbally with husbands. I get husbands to buy diamonds on birthdays. I help them figure out how to be verbal sexually, how to talk about what they like physically, when they have no courage to tell their wives. I help guys recover from divorces. I talk them into not paying for prostitutes and make them feel comfortable about online dating, when that's something they would never have done. I give them advice about their daughters who are teenagers and help them understand when it's right to say something or intervene and do certain things. I do a lot more than dance, and at the end of the day sometimes I'm begged to stay and just to cuddle and get hugged, and not to bummy, stinky, weird degenerates but to very renowned, amazing, awesome, middle-aged guys who haven't been given a long hug in twenty years. And that makes me feel really good and I go out of my way to find those people, and I do all of that as much as I can because it's basically like volunteering. It makes my heart feel great.

Not everyone has had the same experience as Chelsea, and because of that Chelsea has always been a bit of a loner until meeting her "soul sister." She jokes that it only took her twenty years to find her. "I've lived with over 100 girls. I've worked with probably 100,000 girls."[72] There's only one other dancer who she considers her equal spiritually, professionally, and emotionally. "She is completely awake." Not many individuals have the same clarity or vision, which bothers Chelsea, since girls with self-knowledge and foresight are

---

72 Chelsea has worked in some clubs that have hosted 100 shows in one night.

the ones who have the power to change the industry and write their own rules.

> If the girls were able to elevate themselves to a strong state of mind in their early twenties, pimps would go out of business. Raise the caliber. The club will be better. The clubs would expect more from us, and the industry would come back. I just got goose bumps thinking about it. I'm sad about the business and that it's gone, but it can be revived. I have connections with potential investors, and one day I dream of an opportunity to run my own club. I would encourage girls to have a secondary source of income such as a paycheck of any kind, and have benefits available for the girls who want to go to post-secondary. Right now any girl can dance and nothing else matters. I would pick and choose the dancers carefully who would represent my club's identity. The caliber of dancer would be high. My girls would be unattainable, and it would be difficult to believe they even existed outside of the bar, like a mythical creature. I would teach the girls how to do this without giving up their dignity.[73]

Chelsea's wish list for the industry might be a pipe dream, but her strength, perseverance, and mental fortitude enables her to carry that torch. She is not giving up and is determined to do her part to make the scene safe and respectful for everyone involved.

---

73 At the time of publication, Chelsea and her partner, Candice, were co-writing a book about stripping called *Therapist in a Thong* and getting ready to pitch it to publishers.

"The clients are skeety. You have to watch your back if you're working on the street. I've had a gun pulled on me, knife pulled on me. I've had my purse robbed."

Community Perspective
Outreach Interview with Angela Crockwell

Angela Crockwell and I met over coffee at a Jumping Bean on a spring day back in 2015 and had a grand chat about her work, experience, and opinions on matters of prostitution, sex work, and more. Crockwell has worked in outreach for more than thirty years and is the woman behind "It's Nobody's Mandate and Everyone's Responsibility: Sexual Exploitation and the Sex Trade in Newfoundland and Labrador," a report that dives into the dangers and risks associated with prostitution in St. John's and the presence of exploitation in our city.

First tell me what kind of experience you have in outreach and advocacy.

I've been working in the community since the late 80s in a bunch of different roles, but really, primarily with young people, always grassroots, always community-based, always with people living in poverty, people who are marginalized, and so I've done a bunch of different stuff focusing on staying in school, family, education, addictions.

Ok. All different areas.

Yes. Very similar thread. I've been in Shea Heights and Buckmaster's, all low-income neighbourhoods, all grassroots frontline. THRIVE is more broad-based, so very much the same population.

When I volunteered at the Newfoundland and Labrador Sexual Assault Crisis and Prevention Cente (NLSACPC), it really changed the way I looked at things. It stuck with me for a long time, and so I can only imagine how those sorts of things, being involved in those organizations, talking to people, doing that work for decades, how that has affected your view on things and the way you move through your own life.

I think for me there's been a switch from really understanding that there's such a systemic—yes, people face personal barriers, some people have challenges—but there's such a systemic level that keeps people where they are and understanding that we all don't have the same opportunities, and all of us play a role in perpetuating the marginalization of other people whether as parents or as people of society. We all do that to others.

Sometimes, I guess, people don't even realize they're doing it.

I don't think it's intentional. I think that it's systemic; there is a reason why there's inter-generational trauma. There's a reason for that. If you have two kids and both of them struggle in school and one parent can pay for educational assessment and pay for tutoring, and one can't, or a teenager is trying to get a job, and one parent has connections and can make a phone call, and the other… Just those kinds of opportunities, people take for granted. I think, for me, it is recognizing that there is, for most people, this level of privilege that we don't get because it's normal and we all run in similar circles. It's just so normal you just don't get not having access. So the understanding that people are in crisis for often many reasons and that it could be, if you were born in that circumstance, it would be you. It's not an issue of character. It's that it's been their experience.

There are certain circumstances, socioeconomic circumstances, that we all deal with. So what are some services you would see in a dream world? What do you think is really lacking?

Alternative education is lacking significantly, so we still see way too many young people who struggle through that mainstream school system and who drop out.

Is there any alternative education here?

No. We do a series of programs, and then you have the Murphy Centre, and you have some alternatives within the system. What you have is alternative delivery methods, but you don't have alternative curriculum. Everyone still has to follow that standardized way, so I think there should be some significant shifts and opportunities for young people around education. There needs to be shakeup within the child-welfare system, and we need to figure out a much better plan to keep families together. We need better mental-health services. We need better housing. There's all that. If I could say two things, it would be child welfare and education.

It's odd that the education system hasn't evolved. It is interesting that we follow that old-school way?

It was really designed for the Industrial Age, and we haven't radically changed the system.

I never thought about that, but you're right. So, tell me, what are your opinions on sex work in general? Where do you stand?

In terms of do I agree or not agree, good, bad, indifferent?

Wherever you want to go with it.

In 100 percent of my experience, it is a result of vulnerability, trauma, and victimization, so there's a very, very similar path that leads to most people ending up there. I feel really passionate about the respect for—you know it's the same as the high-school crowd or the kid who has a drug addiction or the girl who's working wherever she's working—they're not bad people, you don't need to shame them, you don't need to label them as bad or troubled and delinquent and all of that. They are often victimized, traumatized, and marginalized, and so they're trying to do the best that they can.

So yeah, but I feel very strongly that if you work in prostitution, you're forty times more likely to be murdered than someone who doesn't. It's a highly violent world. It's a place where someone buys you and exploits you, and it's mostly women who are being exploited and mostly men who buy. So you know, I think that the notion that it's okay to go and buy sex from a twenty-year-old woman who has a massive addiction...

Is disgusting.

It is disgusting. Or to go into a strip club and look at the girl up there on the stage who has a history of addiction and violence, and she had to do a line of coke to be able to get on stage. It's not okay. It is not any disrespect to the people who work there. I think often when people speak out against it there's a sense of...there's judgment on the women, and that's not the case.

It's like if you speak out against war, people could assume you don't support the troops, and that's not necessarily true.

Right. That's kind of my stance on that, and to me, most people walk through all the layers, like in the strip club, massage parlour, and out on the street.

Steps?

I know most people who've been in all the places. From my experience most people don't do just one thing. They have been on the street, they've been in massage parlours, they've done inbound calls, they've done outbound calls, they've been in the clubs. It is the world, right? The path that I have seen, I would say it's consistent. If not 100 percent of the time, it's ninety-five percent of the time: early childhood abuse and trauma, family breakdown, on the welfare system, running away, leave home at an early age, valued for sex, exploited maybe through drugs if you do them, not in a non-commercial way, then in a commercial way, then in the adult system. I don't know anybody where that wasn't the path.

That's really horrible.

That's a fact. I don't know anyone where that wasn't a fact.

That says a lot.

So I think, and the research would say, that in Canada the average age to enter the sex trade—yes, there are the forty year olds who are working in the sex trade or the fifty year olds—the average age is fourteen. Also, the biggest risk factor is sexual abuse as children. There are lots of risk factors. There's lots of child welfare, but if you layer sexual abuse and then sexual exploitation, the average age is fourteen. That's the average person's experience. That is how this happens.

I was looking on *Backpages* at some of the pictures of the girls, and it says they're nineteen or twenty, but some of them do not look that age.

No. The notion that, I guess, there are certainly women who would say, "This works for me," or "I want my respect," or "This is dignity work and I want healthcare." Honestly, they can speak for themselves and tell their story.

That's a valuable discussion.

Absolutely. But there's a reason why aboriginal women across this country are so connected with this issue, right? This is not an industry that is made up of, by and large, white privileged people. For me it's really challenging to advocate pro sex work when it is vulnerable people. Then to say, there's nothing wrong with men. Even if you have a woman who is chosen, free choice, had opportunities to be a nurse, a teacher, an early childhood educator, engineer, and had loving parents. When somebody buys, there is no way for them to discern, am I buying somebody who's exploited. You can't do it. So to me, you shouldn't be at it at all . . . and there's a whole discourse that you have the right to choice, respect, health, and so on, but the two worlds are so intertwined you can't. I know one of the people we did a lot of support work with was put on the strip-club circuit.

When you say, put on...

She was moved out of here, IDs taken, cellphone taken.

She was trafficked.

Yeah, she was taken. For the person who is walking into the strip club in Ottawa, she's clean, because you can't be strung out because you won't make as much money. There's no way to look at her and say, there's something wrong there. So the participation in that is victimizing. For me it's a very conscious thing. There are two voices and two experiences, and you either disrespect one or the other, and for a woman to say, "This is my work, I'm pro sex work, I want health insurance, there's nothing wrong with what I do," that's her experience and her story and her right to advocate for that, but every time you say sex work is real work, respectful work, you're dishonouring the vulnerable. I've had young people who've been really, really upset. I've seen them cry in my office, "How can people think that? How can people say what I'm doing is about respect and dignity?" This is trauma and violence. So you disrespect them. When you do research, when academics do research, the people who are in the healthiest place with the most freedom, that's who can contribute to that research, not the fourteen year old who's watched. We're not trying to get somebody into a program, but it's trying to get her in there, out from under the prying hand of her boyfriend who's way older than she is who won't let her move. We need that critical analysis. I understand that I upset people when I say these things, because I'm not honouring someone else's story, but I feel like I'm honouring the majority of the stories. To me, even to go to high-end places where there is safety and where there are rules, vulnerable people don't ever get to work there.

Makes sense.

Like somebody who's really struggling, who's been controlled, who has a serious mental illness, they don't get to work there. They don't get access to that support. So if you only listen to that voice, it's kinda like if you want to get the sense of what it's like to work in the food-service industry and you went and interviewed someone who works at Raymonds. Same thing.

That's a good analogy.

And not realizing most people are working...at McDonald's, and that's a very different experience. That's where most people are.

And that's where most people eat.

Exactly. Yeah, so you know it is a very complicated complex thing, but I just think that if there were opportunities, if there was safety, respect for women. No twelve year old wants to do this. Nobody as a little girl dreams of having to do this.

I heard the other day about a young guy in a school, fourteen-year-old guy here, pimping out some of his friends.

Yeah.

How does that happen? I assume it's an apple from the tree scenario?

Yeah. Exactly. That guy's little girlfriends will be the twenty-five year olds. How does it become okay? It wasn't okay when she was seventeen. How is it okay when she's twenty-five? Poverty sucks, and if you get out of control, and you don't know how you're going to feed yourself and you don't know how you're going to make money and you've done it before and you've crossed that line, you are more likely to go back to it. I certainly know people who as adults have gone back to it, not under the control of anyone, but would say if I hadn't been exploited as a young girl that would never be on the table. I don't know anyone who returns to it when they're well. I know people who return to it when their addictions get out of control and their health is really compromised. When everything falls apart again, they'll go back into it, but when they're well, part of being healthy means not being in that.

Yes. When it comes to Bill C-36, what do you think, in your educated opinion, are the pros and cons?

So for me the pros are: they're trying to target the men and send a message that people aren't for sale, and if we're going to punish anyone in this, it's going to be the buyers and not the workers. I like that. Also, I like that it is recognized that people who are working need understanding and protection and support, and they've tried to target the advertisement of people, really in many ways, the male and exploiter side of the business, but they still won't charge you with prostitution. From a legal standpoint, I'm not anti-bill C-36, but I'm also not a believer that the legal system is ever going to fix or address this because I think it's a social issue. It's like trying to tackle addictions. Criminalizing people with addictions is never going to help. Criminalizing and trying to put up a bunch of walls around this is not really the solution. I don't think we're really going to find the solution here. I think we're going to find the solution in social reform and not legislative reform. If people stop abusing and buying children, the adult industry would be radically changed. If we could only prevent the exploitation and abuse of children, the adult industry would be radically changed, and the amount of people that would be in that system would be significantly reduced. So that's illegal now. It's illegal now. Nobody under the age of eighteen is able to work in the adult system. Look, the police here have long understood that. We have not had significant police interference around this issue, only when they've gotten a lot ofpressure, so only when there's a major issue with stuff happening downtown, and of course they have to respond to those things. I remember one of the former chiefs of police on the radio saying these girls don't need a criminal record, they need support. Right? There's an understanding of that. So you know, people will say, with Bill 36, people will say because communication is illegal you don't get to screen your clients, you can't have a security guard.

Yeah, a material offence.

Yeah, the only person I ever knew with a security guard, the security guard was a pimp, and he got charged with living on the avails of underage girls.

That's a whole other issue.

It's so entwined. The fact that it's illegal to promote. *The Telegram* is running ads, technically they can be charged.

There's something that boggles my mind about that. If it's illegal to advertise, there's all these websites that advertise. It's not hard to find IP addresses and owners. How can they exist?

They're often not exclusively sex. I think the idea is you go after pimps and traffickers because that's who's advertising, and that's where the crime will stop. For some ways, the ideas behind it are out of respect for women and their experience and their trauma and is meant to stop the exploitation. It's so hard to get people. Like if somebody puts up a website or a job or an ad, those girls or women don't necessarily tell on the person who's exploiting them because they're afraid, so there's such an ability to stop that demand, but that's what they're trying to do. I don't have an issue with that. Again for the people that we talk to, the laws are irrelevant because they don't feel the impact of that.

What is the climate like here? How high is the human-trafficking demand here? What are the stats?

There really are no stats because of the way it gets counted and tracked. It's not consistent.

Yeah, it's hard to find any info on that.

What often happens is human trafficking means you have to cross borders, but if I have a girl working for me and I'm her pimp and I move her from St. John's to Mount Pearl, tomorrow night you're in CBS, then you're in Torbay, that's trafficking. It is the exploitation of people. People get much more riled up around trafficking. People can understand and get really into it.

I think people get into it because it's something they understand to be obviously and clearly wrong.

Yeah, it's very clear. And obviously it could be for labour, it could be for other things than sex, but we would see a lot of people that, again, if you have someone who's exploiting you or is moving you, you're trafficked, and that is a very common experience.

What is the relationship between prostitution and homelessness?

There's a definite link. When you think of that vulnerable population, poverty, trauma, if you look at the risk factors for homelessness, they're connected. It's very much the same sort of thing. If you have someone who has nowhere to live, you're banned from every shelter because you went off the rails, now they have to find somewhere to crash, so there are people who are exploited because they need a place to stay. The cost to rent is through the roof, so most people can only afford a bedsitter, and you put a twenty-one-year-old, vulnerable young person, exploited, in a bedsitter where there's no deadbolts on the doors, it gets very much entangled.

It's awful.

Yeah, one of the people that we're working with has not been housed for almost two years. She's been bouncing around and highly exploited.

Do you find doing this type of work emotional or do you feel proud of your work because you think it's important?

I don't find it difficult. At times. There are certain people…it kills you. It breaks your heart. But I've been doing it a long time, so I don't have the same emotional reaction to it like some of it now. I remember the first time I brought a girl into the hospital because she was beaten because she didn't give her boyfriend enough money. It killed me. But after…you get used to it. It's not necessarily desensitized. It should always be tough. It should always be sad. It should always enrage you.

And it's good work.

Yeah, it is. And I don't do a lot of frontline anymore, but I do feel very privileged to do this work and also the social justice slant to it because I could—if I worked in, say, accounting—I would move through this world without a sense of the injustice that goes on, and I'd totally miss it.

You mentioned forced prostitution before. Is there a lot of that happening around here with young people? Is it always an older guy, or is it a slow grooming?

I think there's both. It's not even necessarily slow grooming, but there's definitely grooming and targeting at a younger age. I also think there are things, places, and experiences, that young people find themselves at a party and you have no money and I'll give you drugs but you have to give me a blow job, and you say okay. There's a lot of that. There's a lot of exploiting of vulnerability—you have no other option. If you do this, you'll have access to this. It's exploitation.

Another form of victimization, taking their independence.

Yeah, like people who have no IDs, no anything. Here's how much you make. I know people who've been hospitalized, who have had guns put to their heads. Who have had knives held to their throats, who have been told, if you try to leave I have people in the RNC who are watching you. I'll go after your younger sister.

I was going to ask you if anyone you know, anyone you've counselled, have they died or have you learned after that they've died?

Not in a direct way. I know someone who is dying now. Really she's dying because of health issues because of the work. I don't know anybody who's been murdered.

Suicide?

I know people who have committed suicide and who have been entangled in this life.

I guess you can't say it's because of this.

It's this. It's the addiction, it's the trauma. It's all balled up. I know people who've had multiple suicide attempts, who are struggling with PTSD, people struggle for a very, very, long, long time after this. On a national scale, there's lots of women who are victimized. Look at Pickton and what happened there. If you look at the missing Aboriginal women, this issue is totally linked to that. Women are dying. Absolutely.

Community Perspective
Interview with the Safe Harbour Outreach Project (S.H.O.P.)

This Q&A was done over email.

What are some of the biggest challenges sex workers face? What are the effects of stigma?

After working with over 150 women in Newfoundland who have engaged in sex work, in one form or another, we know the biggest challenge sex workers face is the criminalization of their work. Until sex work is decriminalized, there will always be barriers to sex workers accessing their human rights. The criminalization of sex work certainly lends itself to the stigmatization of sex work and those who do it. Stigma has been named by sex workers in this province, and across Canada, as the worst part of doing sex work. There is a real lack of understanding about sex work and the people who engage in it in our community, and this lack of understanding perpetuates myths, stereotypes, and prejudice, which in turn leads to stigma and discrimination.

Stigma creates real barriers to accessing basic healthcare and housing, to report to the police when they experience violence, to be students, parents, partners, and neighbours, and to live safely and happily in our communities. Stigma creates a social environment in which sex workers (especially women engaged in sex work) are systematically victimized, criminalized, and shamed for experiencing their sexuality in a way that doesn't conform to 'acceptable' sexuality created by mainstream society. This stigma views sex workers as 'bad, immoral people' whose human rights can be dismissed, and who should accept and expect violence. This stigmatization furthers women's isolation and social exclusion, and compromises their dignity and safety. We find this completely unacceptable. Everyone, regardless of their profession, deserves human rights, respect, and safety.

We have the utmost respect for all women we work with, and even when people are in bad situations, we still believe they know what's best for themselves and that things have to happen on their terms, in their own time. Listening to people and believing them leads to the knowledge that there are many people doing sex work, for many reasons, and that everyone's story and situation is different. There is no one truth about sex work or the people that do it.

How can members of the community, government, etc., help lessen or remove these challenges?

First and foremost, we must listen to and believe sex workers and what they have to say about their work and lives. People who want to help can advocate for the full decriminalization of sex work and educate themselves about the realities of sex work. The resources available via the Canadian Alliance for Sex Work Law Reform is a great place to start. We advocate for the human rights of sex workers in Newfoundland and Labrador, and everything we do is guided by the principles of human rights. But what does it mean to come from a human-rights approach to sex work? Let's unpack what that means for the work that we do, the ways we approach the women we work with and why this approach is crucial in supporting women and our communities. Applying a human-rights framework to sex work means:

- Beginning from a place of respect for all people and their autonomy

- Allowing women to define their own lived experiences

- Ensuring basic civil and political rights for meaningful participation in our community

- Rooting the work in the belief that everyone deserves access to human rights, including the right to freedom of expression, association, and movement, supportive healthcare and safe housing, safe and equitable working conditions, and to live and love with dignity and respect

- And recognizing and addressing the ways in which certain groups of people, like sex workers, are denied their human rights due to underlying historical power structures and discrimination based on gender, race, socio-economic class, orientation, ability, citizenship status, ethnicity, family status, and moral judgments

What is SHOP's stance on Bill C-36?

Approaching sex work and sex workers with a commitment to upholding human rights has brought us to advocate for decriminalization of sex work and the repeal of Bill C-36 in Canada, and we aren't the only ones. Sex worker advocacy groups across Canada, often led by sex workers, and many other organizations around the world have listened to sex workers, poured over evidence and research on sex work and human rights and have come to the conclusion that the most supportive thing to do is to call for the decriminalization of sex work. We join the Canadian Alliance for Sex Work Law Reform, the World Health Organization, UNAIDS, the International Labour Organization, the Global Alliance Against Trafficking in Women, the Global Network of Sex Work Projects, the Global Commission on HIV and the Law, Human Rights Watch, the Open Society

Foundations, and Anti-Slavery International and many other sex worker organizations across the world in prioritizing the human rights of all people who engage in sex work, and the decriminalization of sex work. We do this because we know that laws and policing that criminalize sex work expose sex workers to harmful working conditions, marginalize and isolate sex workers, and profoundly decrease their safety, health, and human rights.

What are the pros and cons of sex work being decriminalized or legalized in Canada?

Why decriminalization? We advocate for the full decriminalization of sex work in Canada, rather than the legalization of sex work, along with the provision of supportive, sex worker specific, harm-reduction based community services and programming. The benefits to decriminalization are the ability for people who do sex work to gain full access to their human rights, while still upholding laws against violence including laws against physical and sexual violence, kidnapping, confinement, sexual exploitation, and human trafficking, and age-of-consent laws. The benefits of decriminalization also go beyond sex workers themselves, as decriminalization promotes public health. New Zealand is a great example of decriminalization, and there is significant information available on the positive outcomes there.

Why not legalization? The cited benefits around the legalization of sex work would be that legalizing it would work on decreasing stigma by treating it like any other job, allowing sex workers to unionize, build stronger businesses, and support the national economy through the ability to tax the industry. However, many people across Canada and around the world warn that legalizing sex work may have unintended consequences. In many countries where sex work is legalized, like Germany and within the porn industry in the US, many sex workers are hampered by bureaucratic regulations around where, when, and how sex work takes place. Regulations and intensified government oversight that comes with legalization still criminalizes sex workers who don't comply with regulations. Furthermore this regulation-based approach retains some of the most harmful impacts of past and current laws by disproportionately omitting sex workers who are already marginalized, like people who use drugs, work on the street-level, and who are migrants.

What do you say to anyone who believes sex work should be illegal?

We would ask why they believe that, and ask them to take a step back and consider whether they are basing their thoughts on morals or facts, because the facts show that decriminalization is the most important step we can take towards increasing the human rights and safety of people who do sex work. Decriminalizing sex work still means trafficking and other abuses are illegal. Removing criminal penalties for sex work does *not* remove penalties for exploitation, forced labor, violence, trafficking, rape, or sexual assault—including of minors.

What is your response to those who feel and act as though sex workers have no agency?

When human rights aren't the priority and people's agency is dismissed, we're worried. We're worried because the moral position embedded in the idea that sex workers have no agency does not start from a place of wanting to respectfully understand people and their complex experiences—it starts from a place of telling people who they are and defining what their experiences mean. This silences the voices of people who do consensual sex work, and it's dangerous because it is often used to justify actions that infringe on human rights, and make life more hazardous and unjust for both sex work-ers and people who truly are being exploited. The issue—the biggest part of our worry—is that the beliefs of people taking what is often called the 'rescue approach,' which views all sex work as exploitation in which women engaging in sex work have no agency, are based in moral assumptions around sex work and upholding one truth about the sex industry, rather than the countless realities of the millions of people in this industry. The only way to know about the realities of the sex industry is to listen to those involved in it—this is what those who take a moral-rescue approach to sex work fail to do.

What does it mean to be a sex worker ally?

We know that one experience cannot and should not speak for everyone engaged in sex work, and there is no one truth about sex work, except for the truth that everyone who trades sex deserves human rights. We believe wholeheartedly that being a sex worker ally means first and foremost listening to sex workers and recognizing they are the experts of their own lives. Being a sex worker ally is about working to increase the human rights for sex workers. It is about learning from sex workers and listening to their needs. Being a sex worker ally is about upholding and using the term "sex work," coined and used by sex workers, as a way to rename and define what they do as a form of labour and economic exchange.

Sex workers are much more than the one-dimensional people that stigma makes them out to be. Sex workers are multifaceted people with complex lives. They deserve access to human rights, and they alone are the experts on how to make that happen.

Generally describe the type of people who avail of SHOP's services.

There is no "type of person" who does sex work, and no one "type of person" who avails of our services. Sex workers, as a group of human beings, are as diverse as the general population. SHOP has connected with over 150 sex workers in Newfoundland, and they represent the diversity of our city of St. John's. The women we serve range in age from nineteen to fifty, they come from different backgrounds and different parts of the country. Some are queer and/or trans women, some work as escorts from home, some work on the street, some work part time in massage parlours, some work in local strip clubs, and some have worked in porn.

Many of the women we serve are street-based sex workers engaging in 'survival sex work' and living at the intersections of poverty, homelessness, histories of violence and trauma, dealing with addictions and untreated mental health issues, and trying to survive. We meet them where they are at and support them in working towards the goals they want to achieve, whether that is finding housing or a family doctor, getting on methadone or moving to indoor sex work.

The women we work with are intelligent, resourceful, critical, funny, kind, loving, creative, and come with skills and knowledge that have informed us on our work from the beginning of this program.

What is the relationship between sex work and feminism?

Sex workers have always been at the forefront of social-justice movements, from feminism to LGBTQ rights; however, there are deep tensions between feminism and sex work. Many branches of feminism have denounced the sex-trade industry believing all 'prostitution' is inherently violent and exploitative and that men buying sexual services are committing acts of violence against women. This kind of feminism calls for all forms of sex work to be abolished, as the only way to support and protect women in the industry.

Our feminism includes sex workers, and our feminism values the contributions and leadership of sex workers—and we're happy to say we aren't alone. Many feminists across Canada and across the globe *are* sex workers and sex worker allies, and work towards upholding intersectional feminism that recognizes the diverse experiences of all women, including the realities of sexual exploitation and consensual sex work. Our feminism is about fighting for the safety, participation, and equality of all people—women and men who are trans and cisgender, and non-binary people—including people who sell sex.

What do you say to those who believe sex work is a result of the patriarchy and should be eliminated?

Our goal in a human rights approach is not to eradicate or abolish sex work from our society, as is the case with many anti-human trafficking groups who believe sex work is a result of patriarchy and should be eliminated, and take what can be called a 'rescue' approach to sex work. We see the rescue approach as one that:

- Comes from a moral belief that all trade involving sex and sexual services is wrong and inherently violent

- Labels all people who sell sex to be "victims" who need out side intervention and rescuing, regardless of their conscious and autonomous decisions

- Speaks over and for countless women's experiences and realities, upholding a singular narrative

- Dangerously conflates consensual sex work with sexual exploitation and human trafficking, and conflates the experiences of adults with that of children

- Sees the selling of a sexual service as the selling of a person's entire body and self

- Inconsistently defines what constitutes consent

- Heavily relies on the criminal-justice system, police and government powers to enact justice, often through arrest, criminalization, and incarceration

In strong contrast, our goal is rights, not rescue. We defend and advocate that sex workers rights are human rights. We recognize that sex work is something that many people consent to—whether they work in a strip club, on the street, in a massage parlour, online, in porn, or independently—and they deserve to be able to work and live safely in communities. We also recognize that some people are involved in the sex trade non-consensually, and experience exploitation or human trafficking (when there is sexual exploitation and movement involved), and that those people also deserve access to their human rights. The needs of people who experience exploitation and/or trafficking are vastly different from people who do consensual sex work, but we believe that, no matter what someone's experience of the sex industry, women are the experts of their own lives, and that we must first and foremost listen to them when creating services, supports, policies, or legislation related to sex work. The voice of experience is the most important voice in the conversation, always, and this is the place from which we start our work every day.

Community Perspective
Former Government Worker

Getting government workers to talk to me about the lack of government services for sex workers in need was difficult. Likewise, anyone that worked for Eastern Health could not participate unless they were okay with the risk of getting caught. I found one person who, at one point in life, held a position that had a particular vantage point on homelessness in St. John's. They agreed to participate anonymously. We met for coffee.

What did you do in your line of work?

I helped people find homes and liaised with many shelters across the province such as the Wiseman Centre, Tommy Sexton Center, Iris Kirby House, and the Native Friendship Center.

How was this work done?

Mostly over the phone. An individual would call and basically say, "I'm homeless and need somewhere to stay." We would do an interview and then phone the shelter. Once the stay was approved, the government paid for it. Once the person was in the shelter, the shelter took over.

And then what?

The next step would be to help the person obtain affordable housing, which should be in line with the welfare rate, which was always challenging.

What are the challenges there?

The max rate that is issued for a single person per month for rent is $298, so even though that's the rate, affordable is really $600. So they have to use their individual rate. There are two different rates, the rental rate plus their individual rate, which is supposed to be for food and what not, but most everyone has to dip into their individual just to make rent, and they're left with about $50 a month.

How does this connect to sex workers?

For sex workers who are in this position and are also single mothers, they could be receiving income support and be doing sex work on the side to supplement.

Did you ever knowingly deal with anyone who was doing sex work?

Not in any overt way, but I'm sure some of them were doing that quietly.

What about addictions?

Most had addictions, mental-health issues, criminal backgrounds, have had their children taken from them, had horrible upbringings, or their mothers were sex workers. That's how they grew up. This is how they figured everyone lives. And even though there are people out there helping, they figure this is the way life is, this is how people live.

So do you find it difficult? It sounds like part of what you do could be considered or could feel like enabling.

I would go to bat for some people, and you know, you spend a lot of time and effort trying to get everything in place for them, getting them the support they need, and then you get everything put in place and they turn around and say, "Fuck you," and they go missing for a couple weeks.

Any specific situations come to mind where you would know something was going on but you were really helpless to do anything?

There's one business downtown where an older man who is on disability, he inherited a house that he used to sell girls. He's a pimp pretty much—all the sex he can get, plus they go out and work the streets and make money. They pay rent by giving him sex and he provides crack. We find a lot of the girls we worked with, the pimp is the boyfriend.

Why do you think they are doing it?

Drugs. They needed drugs, and they needed income. They can't work any regular job because Canada Revenue will find out. They need to make big money and quickly. Here we are with all these programs to get people in school, and work, and I mean, so what you can go work in McDonald's and make $12 an hour or you can make $300.

Did you see it often?

There were two girls in and out of the shelters, and they seemed to be doing good, and then one day they just disappeared. A missing-persons report went out. Nothing ever came of it. A few months later we got a phone call from them saying they needed somewhere to stay.

The places, the shelters where you send these girls, I've heard they can be used for recruiting. Is there any truth to that?

It's a breeding ground to get people. They're vulnerable. The counsellors will find out that this girl is recruiting other girls, and she'll be barred from the house for two days. Come back two days later and you're getting three square meals and whatever else goes along with it. They leave that night and go work the streets, and then come back again. It's tough. There's one girl. I was waiting for her to show up dead. She had brain damage because she was beaten so bad in the past. He went to jail, she went into the shelter. He got out. She started working again. Got her ass kicked again. She got locked out. She was back in the shelter.

It sounds like a sad cycle. How does this affect you as someone who is trying to provide assistance?

Sometimes we dealt with horrible things, and we were just supposed to go on like nothing ever happened. It's an impossible situation.[74]

---

[74] At the time of publication a new federally funded program started in St. John's aimed at helping women exit the sex industry.

Legal Perspective
Interview with a Lawyer

This lawyer chose to be anonymous but did get permission from their employer to participate in this project.

What are the current laws on prostitution?

The Code is divided into a variety of sections. Charges relating to Prostitution can be found under Part VII: Disorderly Houses, Gaming and Betting, specifically sections 210 to 213. And Part VIII: Offences against the Person, specifically section 286. There are many other sections of the code that would apply to Prostitution, but these are the sections that specifically deal with sexual services. The law in Canada right now is that any form of buying sexual services is illegal. Advertising sexual services, keeping a bawdy-house (brothel) and/or profiting from sexual services is illegal as well, unless the sexual services are your own.

Can you explain what Bill C-36 is?

The Supreme Court of Canada gave the federal government twelve months to address the laws it deemed unconstitutional in *Canada (Attorney General) v. Bedford* [2013] 3 S.C.R. 1101, 303 C.C.C (3d) 146. The Bill was put in place to amend specific provisions of the criminal code. If the government didn't put any law in place, through the passing of a Bill, there would be no laws on

Prostitution. It is still an anti-prostitution law, and its goal is very clearly stated to protect vulnerable people and victims of sex-trade. The focus is on the buyers, but sellers can also be charged in certain circumstances.

Can you explain what the law states for each of the following:

a. Sex Worker

A sex worker now has immunity from being charged from gaining a material benefit from sexual services, as long as those sexual services are their own; you can sell your own sexual services without being charged. A sex worker can still be charged under sections 210 through 213 as it is illegal to have a bawdy-house, and to advertise yourself in public where it stops or impedes traffic or if the advertisement is near a school, playground, or daycare.

b. Buyer

There are about thirty-plus charges under the Criminal Code that could potentially relate to a buyer. Those charges range from the simple purchase of a sexual service to being involved in human trafficking. There are so many factors relating to what a buyer could be charged with, such as how old the person is that they are buying the sex from, who is getting the money, the level of consent, the place where it happens, any force used, threats, etc. The Criminal Code and Bill C-36 really crack down on anyone being involved in any purchase or profiting of sexual services if you are someone other than the person who "owns" the sexual service. And the sentence associated with these charges range from an Absolute Discharge (a finding of guilt, not a conviction, that leaves you with no criminal record) to Life imprisonment.

What is the legal connection and difference between sex work and human trafficking for sexploitation?

I think it is best for me to address these together. The connection is that both sex work and human trafficking for sexploitation provide sexual services. The difference boils down to consent. Under the

Code, a sex worker who sells sexual services consensually has immunity from being charged. When the Code delves into human trafficking, the person whose sexual services are being used is deemed to be the victim or the complainant. That's a very big difference. On one hand, you have a situation where the sex worker *would* be charged if not for section 286.5 and, on the other, a victim who the government is trying to protect.

Human trafficking involves kidnapping, forcible confinement, threats, etc. It has its own section of the Code, s. 279, and the charges are straight indictable. These are some of the most serious charges in the Code. There would be no suggestion of consent with human trafficking. It would no longer be about "sexual services" in the wording of the charge, but instead it would be sexual assault and aggravated sexual assault.

The focus of the government is to protect those individuals who are providing sexual services without consent or by consent out of desperation. The tricky part is how to know if there is pure consent? The government doesn't appear to believe there is ever real consent.

A separate issue is that anyone under the age of sixteen cannot consent to perform any sexual services, no matter their level of willingness. They would still not be charged within the Code, but the court would deem them a victim as opposed to a willing participant.

What does it mean to live off the avails of sex work?

A financial or material benefit knowing that it is obtained or derived, directly or indirectly, from communication regarding sexual services, advertising sexual services, having those sexual services, or giving sexual services. If a person gets any gain, of any kind whatsoever, from sex work, it would be considered to live off the avails of sex work.

What are the differences between Decriminalization vs. Legalization?

Decriminalization – What was once a criminal offence is no longer a criminal offence. Eliminates the law.

Legislation – Regulates something and creates a framework for when and how it can happen.

Any hypothesis about the future of law in Canada as it relates to prostitution?

The only thing that is clear right now is that sex workers are still not happy with the laws. Selling is now legal, but buying is not. Given the firm hand of the government in Bill C-36, I don't see it becoming legal anytime soon.

Community Resources

EMERGENCY SERVICES

KIDS HELP PHONE
1-800-668-6868

MOBILE CRISIS RESPONSE SERVICE (St. John's Region)
(709) 737-4668

MENTAL HEALTH EMERGENCY SERVICES—
24-hour Province-Wide Mental Health Crisis Phone Line
1-888-737-4668

NEWFOUNDLAND AND LABRADOR SEXUAL ASSAULT CRISIS
AND PREVENTION CENTRE—24 hours
1-800-726-2743 | (709) 747-7757

RNC (Info and Complaints)
(709) 729-8000

SAFE HARBOUR OUTREACH BAD DATE LINE
1-800-726-2743

SUPPORT SERVICES

BLUE DOOR PROGRAM
This program supports individuals, primarily between the ages of fourteen and twenty-nine, to exit sex-trade activities and/or sexually exploitive situations, including sex trafficking. The program is inclusive of gender and sexual orientation. The Blue Door offers intensive, individualized services and supports that address key barriers to the exiting process and helps participants move forward with dignity, self-determination, and respect. Specifically, it focuses on social isolation, complex trauma and mental health, substance use, low literacy/education, employment opportunities, and assistance with accessing safe, affordable housing. In addition, each Blue Door participant can expect to receive individualized intensive support and will have the opportunity to avail of case management

services, exiting skills development, transition planning, and individual therapeutic counselling.

Support Coordinator (709) 754-0536 ext. 212
Support Coordinator (709) 754-0536 ext. 208
Employment and Education Instructor (709) 754-0536 ext. 213
Outreach Facilitator (709) 754-0536 ext. 209

SAFE HARBOUR OUTREACH PROJECT (SHOP)
SHOP exists to advocate for the human rights of sex workers. SHOP provides confidential non-judgmental support to women who have experience with sex work. Call or text to connect to a wide range of services at their sex worker-only space, including one-to-one support, peer drop-ins, public education and training, street outreach, workshop and info sessions, community meals, safer sex and drug use supplies, system navigation, advocacy, and referrals.

(709) 771-7171 | (709) 771-1077
Twitter: @sexworkoutreach
Facebook: facebook.com/SHOP
Drop-in hours: 12pm to 4pm, Tuesday to Thursday
Drop-in dinner: 7pm to 10pm Wednesday

STELLA'S CIRCLE
Stella's Circle is a leading social-services agency in St. John's, NL. They offer programs for adults who have barriers to full participation in the community, including poverty, homelessness, and health issues.

142 Military Road
St. John's, NL, A1C2E6
(709) 738-8390
info@stellascircle.ca | www.stellascircle.ca

STREET REACH
(709) 754-0536

NARCOTICS ANONYMOUS
(709) 728-9084

COALITION AGAINST VIOLENCE
215-31 Peet Street
St. John's, NL
A1B 3W8
(709) 757-0137
cavae.save.now@gmail.com

CORNER BROOK TRANSITION HOUSE
P.O. Box 152
47 Clarence Street
Corner Brook, NL
A2H 6C9
(709) 639-9841

NL HEALTH LINE
811

INCOME SUPPORT/AES (Ages 18-64)
(709) 729-7888

CYFS SOCIAL WORKER (Ages under 18)
(709) 752-4619

THRIVE
(709) 754-0536

CHOICES FOR YOUTH
(709) 754-3047

SAFE WORKS ACCESS PROGRAM (SWAP) at Tommy Sexton Centre
SWAP provides free needles, safe disposal of used needles, sterile water, vitamin C, alcohol prep-pads, safer injecting info, safer crack using stems/straight shooters, brass screens.

47 Janeway Place
Pleasantville
(709) 757-SWAP (7927)
Hours: 8:30am to 4:30pm, Monday to Friday
Arrange delivery: (709) 757-7927

PLANNED PARENTHOOD / NLSHC
(709) 579-1009

WOMEN'S CENTRE
(709) 753-0220

RECOVERY CENTRE
(709) 752-4980

ADULT CENTRAL INTAKE (Ages 18+)
(709) 752-8888

YOUTH CENTRAL INTAKE (Ages up to 17)
(709) 777-2200

NATIONAL HUMAN TRAFFICKING TOLL-FREE LINE
1-866-528-7109

SHELTERS

IRIS KIRBY HOUSE
(709) 753-1492

NAOMI CENTRE (Ages 16-30)
(709) 579-8432

NATIVE FRIENDSHIP CENTRE
(709) 579-5970

TOMMY SEXTON CENTRE
(709) 579-8656

WISEMAN CENTRE (Ages 25-64)
(709) 739-8355

YOUNG MEN'S SHELTER (ages 16-24)
(709) 757-3050

Bibliography

Agustin, Laura. *Sex at the Margins: Migration, Labour Markets and the Rescue Industry*. London: Zed Books, 2007.

Auger, Cheryl. "Bill C-36: No Safety or Security for Sex Workers." *Rabble*. October 17, 2014. http://rabble.ca/news/2014/10/bill-c-36-no-safety-or-security-sex-workers.

Bennett, Darcie. "Canada vs. Bedford: The Decision in 750 Words." *PIVOT*. December 20, 2013. http://www.pivotlegal.org.

Bennett, Jessica. *Feminist Fight Club: An Office Survival Manual for a Sexist Workplace*. New York: HarperCollins, 2016.

Benoit, Cecilia, and Leah Shumka. "Sex Work in Canada." *(Understanding) Sex Work: A Health Research and Community Partnership*. May 7, 2015. http://www.understandingsexwork.com/sites/default/files/uploads/2015%2005%2007%20Benoit%20%26%20Shumka%20Sex%20Work%20in%20Canada_2.pdf.

Boskey, Elizabeth. "The Incubation Period of Common STDs." *Verywell*. June 14, 2016. https://www.verywell.com/how-long-before-std-symptoms-appear-3133026.

Canada Outlaws Prostitution. Video. *RT America*, June 20, 2014. https://www.youtube.com/watch?v=Ow3gG1D9WRA.

Canadian Public Health Association. *Sex Work in Canada: The Public Health Perspective*. Ottawa: Canadian Public Health Association, 2014.

Carvajal, Doreen. "Amnesty International Considers Pushing for Decriminalization of Prostitution." *The New York Times*. July 31, 2015. http://www.nytimes.com/2015/08/01/world/europe/amnesty-international-weighs-decriminalization-of-prostitution.html?_r=0.

Chateauvert, Melinda. *Sex Workers Unite: A History of the Movement from Stonewall to Slutwalk*. Boston: Beacon Press, 2013.

Chen, Michele. "Canada's New Law is Forcing Sex Workers onto the Streets and into Harm's Way." *The Nation*. January 29, 2015. https://www.thenation.com/article/canadas-new-law-forcing-sex-workers-streets-and-harms-way.

Coalition Against the Sexual Exploitation of Youth (CASEY). "It's Nobody's Mandate and Everyone's Responsibility: Sexual Exploitation and the Sex Trade in Newfoundland and Labrador." St. John's: Community Youth Network, April 2011. http://www.exec.gov.nl.ca/exec/wpo/publications/STR.pdf.

Delacoste, Frederique, and Priscilla Alexander eds. *Sex Work: Writings by Women in the Sex Industry.* Pittsburgh: Cleis Press, 1998.

Elizabeth, Nicole. "Support, Supplies & Sex Work Allies: Talking S.H.O.P. with Laura Winters." *Secret East.* November 14, 2014. http://secreteast.ca/2014/11/support-supplies-sex-work-allies-talking-s-h-o-p-with-laura-winters.

"Erotic massage parlour moratorium applauded by youth outreach group." *CBC News.* February 25, 2015. http://www.cbc.ca/news/canada/newfoundland-labrador/erotic-massage-parlour-moratorium-applauded-by-youth-outreach-group-1.2970971.

Favor Hamilton, Suzy. *Fast Girl: A Life Spent Running from Madness.* New York: HarperCollins, 2015.

Ferris, Shawna. *Street Sex Work and Canadian Cities: Resisting a Dangerous Order.* Edmonton: University of Alberta Press, 2015.

Foucault, Michel. *The History of Sexuality, Volume 1: An Introduction.* Trans. Robert Hurley. New York: Vintage, 1978.

Fox, Shell, and Andy Braginsky. *Prostitution in Canada: A Short Documentary.* Documentary. September 29, 2015. https://www.youtube.com/watch?v=XQNzputtOmI.

"Gang rape warning issued for St. John's sex workers." *CBC News.* October 3, 2014. http://www.cbc.ca/news/canada/newfoundland-labrador/gang-rape-warning-issued-for-st-john-s-sex-workers-1.2785970.

Gay, Roxane. *Bad Feminist.* New York: HarperCollins, 2014.

Government of Canada Department of Justice. *Technical Paper: Bill C-36, Protection of Communities and Exploited Persons Act.* March 10, 2015. http://www.justice.gc.ca/eng/rp-pr/other-autre/protect/p1.html.

Grant, Melissa Gira. *Playing the Whore: The Work of Sex Work.* London: Verso, 2014.

Guindon, Andre. *The Sexual Language: An Essay in Moral Theology.* Ottawa: University of Ottawa Press, 1976.

Hersh, Lauren. "Prostitution is Not Just Another Job." *The Huffington Post.* March 29, 2016. http://www.huffingtonpost. com/lauren-hersh/prostitution-is-not-just-_b_9557032.html.

Hill, Frances. *A Delusion of Satan: The Full Story of the Salem Witch Trials.* Boston: Da Capo Press, 1997.

Hoff Sommers, Christina. *The War Against Boys: How Misguided Policies are Harming our Young Men.* New York: Simon and Schuster, 2000.

Jeffrey, Leslie Ann, and Gayle MacDonald eds. *Sex Workers in the Maritimes Talk Back.* Vancouver: UBC Press, 2006.

Jervis, Lisa, and Andi Zeisler eds. *Bitchfest: Ten Years of Cultural Criticism from the Pages of Bitch Magazine.* New York: Farrar, Straus and Giroux, 2006.

Jones, Rashida. *Hot Girls Wanted.* Documentary. Directed by Jill Bauer and Ronna Gradus. Two to Tangle Productions, 2015.

Kraig, Donald Michael. *Modern Sex Magick: Secrets of Erotic Spirituality.* St. Paul, MN: LLewllyn Publications, 1998.

Leigh, Carol. "Gloria Steinem, Sex Workers and the Harms of Feminism." *Storify.* March 2015. https://storify.com/ carolleigh/gloria-steinem-a-swerf.

McNulty, Johnny. "Sex workers share stories of the strangest clients they've encountered in the line of booty." *Someecards.* April 4, 2016. http://www.someecards.com/love/sex/sex-worker-stories.

Moran, Caitlin. *How to be a Woman.* New York: HarperCollins, 2011.

Murphy, Catherine, Policy Advisor at Amnesty International. "Sex Workers Rights are Human Rights." *Amnesty International.* August 14, 2015. https://www.amnesty.org/en/latest/news/ 2015/08/sex-workers-rights-are-human-rights.

Neuwirth, Jessica. "Sex workers to fight any NSW register amid claims it creates stigma." *The Guardian*. September 6, 2015. https://www.theguardian.com/society/2015/sep/06/sex-workers-to-fight-any-nsw-register-amid-claims-it-creates-stigma.

"Newfoundland and Labrador Initiatives on Human Trafficking." *Sisters of Mercy of Newfoundland*. July 31, 2012. http://www.sistersofmercynf.org/news/view_article.cfm?loadref=33&id=64.

"Nine sex workers take part in interviews with RNC." *CBC News*. October 23, 2015. http://www.cbc.ca/news/canada/newfoundland-labrador/9-sex-workers-take-part-in-interviews-with-rnc-1.3286182.

NL Coalition Against Human Trafficking Inc. "The Global Slave Trade in NL." Conference Report, St. John's, April 7-9, 2014. Published June 2014.

Parliament of Canada. *House Government Bill - Bill C-36 - Royal Assent (41-2)*. Ottawa, ON, November 6, 2014. http://www.parl.gc.ca/HousePublications/Publication.aspx?Mode=1&DocId=6767128&Col=1&Language=E&File=4.

Perrin, Benjamin. *How to Make Canada's New Prostitution Laws Work*. Ottawa: MacDonald-Laurier Institute, October 2014.

Pelley, Chad. "'Why You Should Want 'Adult Massage Parlours' Like Kendra's Red House in Your City." *The Overcast*. March 2, 2015. http://theovercast.ca/want-adult-massage-parlours-like-kendras-red-house-city.

Pinker, Susan. *The Sexual Paradox: Extreme Men, Gifted Women and the Real Gender Gap*. Toronto: Vintage, 2009.

"Prostitution charges hit zero as enforcement focus shifts: RNC, RCMP approach prioritizes communication, safety in the N.L. sex trade." *CBC News*. January 28, 2014. http://enforcement-focus-shifts-1.2513007.

Ratchford, Sarah. "Canada's New Sex Work Laws Are Taking a Big Step Backwards." *Vice*. June 6, 2014. https://www.vice.com/en_ca/article/canadas-new-sex-work-laws-are-taking-a-big-step-backwards.

Ratchford, Sarah. "Two Weeks After Newfoundland's Alleged Gang Rapes, Still No Investigation. Here's Why." *Vice*. January 11, 2015. http://www.vice.com/en_ca/read/two-weeks-after-new-foundlands-alleged-gang-rapes-still-no-investigation-heres-why-932.

Ryan, Christopher, and Cecilia Jethá. *Sex at Dawn: How We Mate, Why We Stray, and What It Means for Modern Relationships*. New York: Knopf, 2010.

Showden, Carisa R., and Samantha Majic eds. *Negotiating Sex Work: Unintended Consequences of Policy and Activism*. Minneapolis: University of Minnesota Press, 2014.

Smith, Tyler Stoddard. *Whore Stories: A Revealing History of the World's Oldest Profession*. Massachusetts: Adams Media, 2012.

Stanger, Elle. "I'm a Sex Worker, and This is What I'll Tell My Child." *Elephant Journal*. March 18, 2016. http://www.ele-phantjournal.com/2016/03/im-a-sex-worker-and-this-is-what-ill-tell-my-child.

Steinem, Gloria. *My Life on the Road*. New York: Random House, 2015.

"SWAP Harm Reduction Training Module." Developed by ACNL/SWAP, May 2006. Revised October 2015.

Sweet, Barb. "Residents wonder how massage parlour got approval." *The Telegram*. February 25, 2015. http://www.thetelegram.com/News/Local/2015-02-25/article-4055927/Residents-wonder-how-massage-parlour-got-approval/1.

Tani, Maxwell. "Sex Worker Explains the Difference between Legalizing and Decriminalizing Prostitution." *Business Insider*. June 10, 2015. http://www.businessinsider.com/sex-worker-explains-the-difference-between-legalizing-and-decriminalizing-prostitution-2015-6.

"The law and massage parlours," *The Telegram*. February 25, 2015. http://www.thetelegram.com/News/Local/2015-02-25/article-4056781/The-law-and-massage-parlours/1.

Van der Meulen, Emily, Elya M. Durisin, and Victoria Love. *Selling Sex: Experience, Advocacy, and Research on Sex Work in Canada.* Vancouver: UBC Press, 2013.

"Violent John Reported by Sex Workers in Downtown St. John's." *CBC News.* February 26, 2016. http://www.cbc.ca/news/ canada/newfoundland-labrador/shop-warning-sex-workers-1.3465876.

Walsh, Adam, and Jen White. "Grim tales of the sex trade reveal need for support: 2 former workers describe their experiences and struggles to stay out of the business." *CBC News.* May 8, 2013. http://www.cbc.ca/news/canada/newfoundland-labrador/grim-tales-of-the-sex-trade-reveal-need-for-support-1.1307530.

White, Jen. "Sex trade workers in high demand in N.L.: Influx of escorts travelling to province, as business shifts from streets to web." *CBC News.* May 7, 2013. www.cbc.ca/news/canada/ newfoundland-labrador/sex-trade-workers-in-high-demand-in-n-l-1.1307533.

"Wild Sex Series: Prostitution." Ep 12. Video. *Earth Touch TV.* February 6, 2013. https://www.youtube.com/watch?v= DA0E3EkGusk.

Wolf, Naomi. *Promiscuities: The Secret Struggle for Womanhood.* Toronto: Vintage, 1998.

Acknowledgments

MANY THANKS TO Gerard Collins, Mike Heffernan, Julia Day, Wendy Goldman-Rohm, Laura Barron, Dublin Writers Workshop, Pipers Frith, Chris Hickey, Newfoundland and Labrador Arts Council, Chad Pelley, Breakwater Books, Blue Door Program, Angela Crockwell, Street Reach, and The Safe Harbour Outreach Project.

This book would not be possible without the involvement of many anonymous contributors from all walks of life. Thank you.

Thank you to my husband, all my family, friends, and coworkers for your relentless support.

KERRI CULL has a graduate degree in English from Memorial University of Newfoundland and is the founder of the former *Book Fridge* blog for which she interviewed writers and reviewed a few hundred books over a two-year span. She has written for a handful of newspapers and magazines, has authored one book of poetry, *Soak* (2012), and is currently working on a novel. She lives and works in St. John's.